3-95

3-18-64

(61-12221)

TO TURN THE TIDE

PRESIDENT JOHN F. KENNEDY

A SELECTION FROM PRESIDENT KENNEDY'S PUBLIC

STATEMENTS FROM HIS ELECTION THROUGH THE

1961 ADJOURNMENT OF CONGRESS, SETTING FORTH

THE GOALS OF HIS FIRST LEGISLATIVE YEAR

TO TURN THE TIDE

Edited by John W. Gardner

Foreword by Carl Sandburg

Introduction by President Kennedy

Harper & Row, Publishers
New York, Evanston, and London

TO TURN THE TIDE

A-O

CONTENTS

Contents

EDITOR'S NOTE

This book contains a selection of President Kennedy's speeches and writings from election through his first legislative year. The first year of a President's term is of more than ordinary interest. In that year he sets the tone and style of his Administration, and in large part formulates the goals that will concern him throughout his years in the White House.

This is not a history of the first legislative year. Nor is it a comprehensive collection of the President's official communications during that year. It is a selection of the most important things the President had to say about the issues we face as a nation. In 1961 the gravest of these issues were international, and the selection of materials for inclusion in the book reflects that reality.

President Kennedy has an extraordinary capacity to express himself in speech and in writing. Rarely has an American President stated the nation's problems with such clarity, or voiced its aspirations so movingly. The reader of these pages runs no danger of getting entangled in thickets of bureaucratic prose. He will find here a lucid, instructive and eloquent introduction to the problems facing a great nation in a troubled century.

The appendix contains a chronological list of the speeches and writings quoted in the book. The list indicates the pages on which the various items appear, and also indicates whether the item appears in full or only in excerpts.

I wish to thank Rosalinde B. Kaufman, Lonnie A. Sharpe, Evan Thomas and John Fischer for their assistance at various stages of the book.

JOHN W. GARDNER

FOREWORD

The White House, 1600 Pennsylvania Avenue, Washington, D.C., holds more interesting ghosts than any other house in our country. All the past Presidents except George Washington have lived, slept and toiled here and written counsels for their own and later generations. Nearly all great soldiers and distinguished commanders have reported here. The great figures of Senate and House came here to meet with other men of the government. The architects of our national structure speak here in their many phantom voices. Leafing our way through this book we may believe that John Fitzgerald Kennedy has communed with many of these phantoms. He is deeply immersed in the past, searching it for lights it may throw on the confused present and the inscrutable future.

From day to day and midnight to midnight the President looks out at the multiple mirrors of the changing chaos of global history. By mail, phone, radio, TV, by wire, cable, messenger, it comes to the White House in fact, flying rumor, official communiqué, guesses, probabilities and possibilities often weaving crazy and dizzy patterns. Never between world wars have public report and private rumor dealt with so many known factors overbalanced by the unknown.

The President is the Head Watchman of "government of the people, by the people, for the people." His every sentence, every spoken or written word goes to the eyes, ears, minds of millions of people reading or listening. The People?

Born with bones and heart fused in deep and violent secrets
Mixed from a bowl of sky blue dreams and sea slime facts—

A seething of saints and sinners, toilers, loafers, oxen, apes
In a womb of superstition, faith, genius, crime, sacrifice—
The one and only source of armies, navies, work-gangs,
The living flowing breath of the history of nations,
Of the little Family of Man hugging the little ball of Earth,
And a long hall of mirrors, straight, convex and concave,
Moving and endless with scrolls of the living,
Shimmering with phantoms flung from the past,
Shot over with lights of babies to come, not yet here.

Besides the President's toils and decisions for the present generations, some of his work will reach people George Washington called "the unborn millions," those Lincoln termed "the remotest generation."

In his House Divided speech Lincoln said, "If we could first know where we are and whither we are tending we could better judge what to do and how to do it." So here we have, in a book of speeches and messages of our President, a colossal survey of America and its people, their human conditions, their problems that must be faced, the terrific complications overseas and around the globe. He presents the known facts as to where we are and whither we are tending and offers his counsel on what to do and how to do it.

Not often has a President of our country had, besides content and substance in his speeches, the further merit of style as such. We recur to Jefferson, Lincoln, Wilson, the two Roosevelts, and we are near the end of the list. In the opinion of many, Kennedy belongs among those always having good solid content, often color and cadence in style, and there are moments in the cause of human freedom when his words move with a measured passion.

If he speaks to the country, there are those who are sure he has said just the right thing and others sure that once more he has opened his mouth to no use and avail. If he says nothing, there are those who are sure he will speak in the future at the precise hour when his words will count, while others are sure that either his silence is significant and connects with his ignorance and vacillation or he is holding back and keeping secret important matters he should be telling the country about. If he opens any door of policy, he is sure to hear it should be opened wider, it should be closed entirely, or there should be a new door or a return to the door that was there before, or the original intention of the Founding Fathers was that a window is better than a door anyhow.

Fifty years ago on a Chicago streetcar I heard a woman explain to a child, "The President lives in the White House in Washington, where he signs bills they bring him, and he can do anything he wants to so long as they don't stop him." And high-priced constitutional lawyers can't frame a more accurate description in the same number of plain words.

In our nuclear era our weapons are intricate to a fantastic degree. Theaters of operation include sea bottom and stratosphere, the floor of the ocean, the top of the sky. From the man in the White House must come decisions. Every hour he says Yes or No or Perhaps or Not-yet or "We can't see that far." Is it possible for anyone outside of that place of authority to know what it is like inside? With every clock tick he moves under tangled and invisible burdens, dark and involved thongs and pressures.

The Inaugural Address of President Kennedy is a manner of summons to citizens by the new head of our great Republic. Around nearly every sentence of it could be written a thesis, so packed is it with implications. There is drama in such affirmations as: "I have sworn before you and Almighty God the same solemn oath our forebears prescribed nearly a century and three-quarters ago. The world is very different now. For man holds in his mortal hands the power to abolish all forms of human poverty and all forms of human life."

Later came his message to Congress on the State of the Union. Here we have history in a panorama of fact. In our time of terrific storm, unprecedented change, humanity at a crossroads amid endless forked lightning, these pages have in effect answered the questions, "Where are we now?"—"Where do we go from here?"—"How do you look at it?" Soberly, even somberly, we read and linger over Kennedy's words to the Congress: "Before my term has ended, we shall have to test anew whether a nation organized and governed such as ours can endure. The outcome is by no means certain. The answers are by no means clear. All of us together—this Administration, this Congress, this nation—must forge those answers. . . . No man entering upon this office, regardless of his party, regardless of his previous service in Washington, could fail to be staggered upon learning, even in this brief ten-day period, the harsh enormity of the trials through which we must pass in the next four years."

At the United Nations he sketches "the Communist empire" as having "governments installed by foreign troops instead of free institutions, under a system which knows only one party and one belief, which suppresses free debate, free election, free newspapers, free books and free trade unions, and which builds a wall to keep truth a stranger and its own citizens prisoners." Many sentences here can be lingered over: "The events and decisions of the next ten months may well decide the fate of man for the next ten thousand years." "Today, every inhabitant of this planet must contemplate the day when it may no longer be habitable. Every man, woman and child lives under a nuclear sword of Damocles, hanging by the slenderest of threads, capable of being cut at any moment by accident, miscalculation or madness. The weapons of war must be abolished before they abolish us."

We could go on and on quoting from pages herein dealing with dark crossroads, pages sometimes having bursts of light and hope and always the composure that goes with true courage.

Plainly he has had humility, scruples, care and anxiety about what he thinks, writes and says, hoping to mislead no one, hoping his words will stand up and make sense and perhaps wisdom for his own time and later times. When our generation has passed away, when the tongues of praise and comment now speaking have turned to a cold dumb dust, it will be written that John F. Kennedy walked with the American people in their vast diversity and gave them all he had toward their moving on into new phases of their great human adventure.

CARL SANDBURG

INTRODUCTION

The White House,
November 8, 1961

One year ago today the campaign ended. A new endeavor began. Not all, by any means, of the crises and choices which crowded these last twelve months are reflected in the pages that follow. We live in an age when the conduct of foreign affairs consists of more than "open covenants openly arrived at"—and when the details of many programs, foreign and domestic, are too complex or technical for a speech or book that is directed to a wider audience.

Nevertheless John Gardner and Harper & Brothers have ably collected in one volume those speeches and messages of the past twelve months which best sum up, in their judgment, the chief programs and problems of this Administration.

Mr. Gardner undertook a difficult, if not insuperable, task: to strike the proper balance between foreign and domestic issues, to make this collection comprehensive without being tedious, and to preserve those materials which will be of interest to contemporary readers as well as future researchers. The extent to which he succeeded must be decided by each individual reader; in my judgment he has captured the main thrust of our efforts at home and abroad.

The words of any occupant of this office—particularly his words on foreign policy—are certain to be heard and likely to be acted upon by more than one audience: adversaries, allies, neutrals, the Congress, and other members of the Administration as well as all the diverse individuals and interest groups which compose the American electorate. Each must be taken into account. A boon to one may be a bane to others. No group can later be assured privately that words broadcast to all were meant only for some, or were not intended to mean what they clearly seemed to say.

Every Presidential decision, as noted above, cannot be immediately revealed in a major speech, and every Presidential speech cannot reveal a major decision. But the speeches contained in this collection—addressed to the Congress, to the United Nations, or to the American people—represent in most cases days, weeks or months of decision-making within the Administration, and often served as a means of completing as well as conveying those decisions.

Strong words alone, of course, do not make meaningful policy; they must, in foreign affairs in particular, be backed both by a will and by weapons that are equally strong. Thus a collection of Presidential statements cannot convey their true perspective unless it is realized or recalled precisely what they signified in committing the power and majesty of the American people and government.

Words can do more than convey policy. They can also convey and create a mood, an attitude, an atmosphere—or an awakening. In 1961 the American people awakened as never before to a sober realization of the perils that beset our nation. Early complaints about the harsh sound of candor in the place of complacency gave way to a grim determination to do whatever had to be done to preserve both peace and freedom. There has also been a growing recognition that we must fit our power to our responsibilities, and that those tasks which are within our hopes and hopefully within our power cannot all be "finished in the first hundred days . . . nor even perhaps in our lifetime on this planet."

But we have begun. Neither wind nor tide is always with us. Our course on a dark and stormy sea cannot always be clear. But we have set sail—and the horizon, however cloudy, is also full of hope.

JOHN F. KENNEDY

TO TURN THE TIDE

CHAPTER I
OVERTURE

". . . OF THOSE TO WHOM MUCH IS GIVEN, MUCH IS REQUIRED."

"LET EVERY NATION KNOW . . . THAT WE SHALL PAY ANY PRICE, BEAR ANY BURDEN . . . SUPPORT ANY FRIEND, OPPOSE ANY FOE TO ASSURE THE SURVIVAL . . . OF LIBERTY."

"ALL THIS WILL NOT BE FINISHED IN THE FIRST ONE HUNDRED DAYS. NOR WILL IT BE FINISHED IN THE FIRST ONE THOUSAND DAYS, NOR IN THE LIFE OF THIS ADMINISTRATION, NOR EVEN PERHAPS IN OUR LIFETIME ON THIS PLANET. BUT LET US BEGIN."

On January 9, 1961, eleven days before he was to take office, the President-Elect addressed the Massachusetts Legislature. Speaking on his home ground, among men who had known him all his political life, and his father and grandfather before him, Mr. Kennedy spoke movingly of the past and the future.

THE YEARS AHEAD

*Speech to the Massachusetts State Legislature,
January 9, 1961*

I have welcomed the opportunity to address this historic body, and, through you, the people of Massachusetts, to whom I am so deeply indebted for a lifetime of friendship and trust. For fourteen years I have placed my confidence in the voters of this state, and they have generously responded by placing their confidence in me.

Now, on the Friday after next, I am to assume new and broader responsibilities. But I am not here to bid farewell to Massachusetts. For forty-three years, whether I was in London, Washington, the South Pacific or elsewhere, this has been my home; and, God willing, wherever I serve, it will always remain my home.

It was here my grandparents were born; it is here I hope my grandchildren will be born.

I speak neither from false provincial pride nor artful political flattery. For no man about to enter high public office in this country can ever be unmindful of the contributions this state has made to our national greatness. Its leaders have shaped our destiny since long before the great Republic was born. Its principles have guided our footsteps in times of crisis as well as calm. Its democratic institutions, including this historic body, have served as beacon lights for other nations as well as your sister states. For what Pericles said of the Athenians has long been true of this Commonwealth: "We do not imitate, but are a model to others."

And so it is that I carry with me from this state to that high and lonely office to which I now succeed more than fond memories and fast friendships. The enduring qualities of Massachusetts—the common threads woven by the Pilgrim and the Puritan, the fisherman and the farmer, the Yankee and the immigrant—will not be and could not be forgotten in the nation's Executive Mansion. They are an indelible part of my life, my convictions, my view of the past, my hopes for the future.

Allow me to illustrate: During the last sixty days, I have been engaged in the task of constructing an Administration. It has been a long and deliberate process. Some have counseled greater speed. Others have counseled more expedient tests. But I have been guided by the standard John Winthrop set before his shipmates on the flagship *Arbella* 331 years ago, as they, too, faced the task of building a government on a new and perilous frontier. "We must always consider," he said, "that we shall be as a city upon a hill—the eyes of all people are upon us."

Today, the eyes of all people are truly upon us, and our governments, in every branch, at every level, national, state and local, must be as a city upon a hill, constructed and inhabited by men aware of their grave trust and their great responsibilities. For we are setting out upon a voyage in 1961 no less hazardous than that undertaken by the *Arbella* in 1630. We are committing ourselves to tasks of statecraft no less awesome than that of governing the Massachusetts Bay Colony, beset as it then was by terror without and disorder within.

History will not judge our endeavors, and a government cannot be selected, merely on the basis of color or creed or even party affiliation. Neither will competence and loyalty and stature, while essential to the utmost, suffice in times such as these.

For of those to whom much is given, much is required. And when at some future date the high court of history sits in judgment on each of us, recording whether in our brief span of service we fulfilled our responsibilities to the state, our success or failure, in whatever office we hold, will be measured by the answers to four questions:

First, were we truly men of courage, with the courage to stand up to one's enemies, and the courage to stand up, when necessary, to one's associates, the courage to resist public pressure as well as private greed?

Second, were we truly men of judgment, with perceptive judgment of the future as well as the past, of our own mistakes as well as the mistakes of others, with enough wisdom to know what we did not know, and enough candor to admit it?

Third, were we truly men of integrity, men who never ran out on either the principles in which we believed or the people who believed in us, men whom neither financial gain nor political ambition could ever divert from the fulfillment of our sacred trust?

Finally, were we truly men of dedication, with an honor mortgaged to no single individual or group, and compromised by no private obligation or aim, but devoted solely to serving the public good and the national interest?

Courage, judgment, integrity, dedication—these are the historic qualities of the Bay Colony and the Bay State, the qualities which this state has consistently sent to Beacon Hill here in Boston and to Capitol Hill back in Washington. And these are the qualities which, with God's help, this son of

Massachusetts hopes will characterize our government's conduct in the four stormy years that lie ahead. Humbly I ask His help in this undertaking; but aware that on earth His will is worked by men, I ask for your help and your prayers as I embark on this new and solemn journey.

INAUGURAL ADDRESS

As many thousands of visitors converged on Washington for the Inauguration, a blizzard struck the Eastern seaboard and all but paralyzed transportation. The streets of Washington were clogged with snow and stranded automobiles, but the Inaugural ceremony went on as scheduled, and the new President delivered a memorable address.

Inaugural Address,
January 20, 1961

We observe today not a victory of party but a celebration of freedom, symbolizing an end as well as a beginning, signifying renewal as well as change. For I have sworn before you and Almighty God the same solemn oath our forebears prescribed nearly a century and three-quarters ago.

The world is very different now. For man holds in his mortal hands the power to abolish all forms of human poverty and all forms of human life. And yet the same revolutionary belief for which our forebears fought is still at issue around the globe, the belief that the rights of man come not from the generosity of the state but from the hand of God.

We dare not forget today that we are the heirs of that first revolution. Let the word go forth from this time and place, to friend and foe alike, that the torch has been passed to a new generation of Americans, born in this century, tempered by war, disciplined by a hard and bitter peace, proud of our ancient heritage, and unwilling to witness or permit the slow undoing of those human rights to which this nation has always been committed, and to which we are committed today at home and around the world.

Let every nation know, whether it wishes us well or ill, that we shall pay any price, bear any burden, meet any hardship, support any friend, oppose any foe to assure the survival and the success of liberty.

This much we pledge—and more.

To those old allies whose cultural and spiritual origins we share, we pledge the loyalty of faithful friends. United, there is little we cannot do in a host of co-operative ventures. Divided, there is little we can do, for we dare not meet a powerful challenge at odds and split asunder.

To those new states whom we welcome to the ranks of the free, we pledge our word that one form of colonial control shall not have passed away merely to be replaced by a far more iron tyranny. We shall not always expect to find them supporting our view. But we shall always hope to find them strongly supporting their own freedom, and to remember that, in the past, those who foolishly sought power by riding the back of the tiger ended up inside.

To those peoples in the huts and villages of half the globe struggling to break the bonds of mass misery, we pledge our best efforts to help them help themselves, for whatever period is required, not because the Communists may be doing it, not because we seek their votes, but because it is right. If a free society cannot help the many who are poor, it cannot save the few who are rich.

To our sister republics south of our border, we offer a special pledge: to convert our good words into good deeds, in a new alliance for progress, to assist free men and free governments in casting off the chains of poverty. But this peaceful revolution of hope cannot become the prey of hostile powers. Let all our neighbors know that we shall join with them to oppose agression or subversion anywhere in the Americas. And let every other power know that this hemisphere intends to remain the master of its own house.

To that world assembly of sovereign states, the United Nations, our last best hope in an age where the instruments of war have far outpaced the instruments of peace, we renew our pledge of support: to prevent it from becoming merely a forum for invective, to strengthen its shield of the new and the weak, and to enlarge the area in which its writ may run.

Finally, to those nations who would make themselves our adversary, we offer not a pledge but a request: that both sides begin anew the quest for peace, before the dark powers of destruction unleashed by science engulf all humanity in planned or accidental self-destruction.

We dare not tempt them with weakness. For only when our arms are sufficient beyond doubt can we be certain beyond doubt that they will never be employed.

But neither can two great and powerful groups of nations take comfort from our present course—both sides overburdened by the cost of modern weapons, both rightly alarmed by the steady spread of the deadly atom, yet both racing to alter that uncertain balance of terror that stays the hand of mankind's final war.

So let us begin anew, remembering on both sides that civility is not a sign of weakness, and sincerity is always subject to proof. Let us never negotiate out of fear, but let us never fear to negotiate.

Let both sides explore what problems unite us instead of belaboring those problems which divide us.

Let both sides, for the first time, formulate serious and precise proposals for the inspection and control of arms, and bring the absolute power to destroy other nations under the absolute control of all nations.

Let both sides seek to invoke the wonders of science instead of its terrors. Together let us explore the stars, conquer the deserts, eradicate disease, tap the ocean depths and encourage the arts and commerce.

Let both sides unite to heed in all corners of the earth the command of Isaiah to "undo the heavy burdens . . . [and] let the oppressed go free."

And if a beachhead of co-operation may push back the jungle of suspicion, let both sides join in creating a new endeavor, not a new balance of power, but a new world of law, where the strong are just and the weak secure and the peace preserved.

All this will not be finished in the first one hundred days. Nor will it be finished in the first one thousand days, nor in the life of this Administration, nor even perhaps in our lifetime on this planet. But let us begin.

In your hands, my fellow citizens, more than mine, will rest the final success or failure of our course. Since this country was founded, each generation of Americans has been summoned to give testimony to its national loyalty. The graves of young Americans who answered the call to service surround the globe.

Now the trumpet summons us again—not as a call to bear arms, though arms we need; not as a call to battle, though embattled we are; but a call to bear the burden of a long twilight struggle, year in and year out, "rejoicing in hope, patient in tribulation," a struggle against the common enemies of man: tyranny, poverty, disease and war itself.

Can we forge against these enemies a grand and global alliance, North and South, East and West, that can assure a more fruitful life for all mankind? Will you join in that historic effort?

In the long history of the world, only a few generations have been granted the role of defending freedom in its hour of maximum danger. I do not shrink from this responsibility; I welcome it. I do not believe that any of us would exchange places with any other people or any other generation. The energy, the faith, the devotion which we bring to this endeavor will light our country and all who serve it, and the glow from that fire can truly light the world.

And so, my fellow Americans, ask not what your country can do for you; ask what you can do for your country.

My fellow citizens of the world, ask not what America will do for you, but what together we can do for the freedom of man.

Finally, whether you are citizens of America or citizens of the world, ask of us here the same high standards of strength and sacrifice which we ask of you. With a good conscience our only sure reward, with history the final judge of our deeds, let us go forth to lead the land we love, asking His blessing and His help, but knowing that here on earth God's work must truly be our own.

CHAPTER II
PERIL AND OPPORTUNITY

"WE HAVE NO GREATER ASSET THAN THE WILLINGNESS OF A FREE AND DETERMINED PEOPLE, THROUGH ITS ELECTED OFFICIALS, TO FACE ALL PROBLEMS FRANKLY AND MEET ALL DANGERS FREE FROM PANIC OR FEAR."

"WHERE NATURE MAKES NATURAL ALLIES OF US ALL, WE CAN DEMONSTRATE THAT BENEFICIAL RELATIONS ARE POSSIBLE EVEN WITH THOSE WITH WHOM WE MUST DEEPLY DISAGREE, AND THIS MUST SOMEDAY BE THE BASIS OF WORLD PEACE AND WORLD LAW."

"LET IT BE CLEAR THAT THIS ADMINISTRATION RECOGNIZES THE VALUE OF DISSENT AND DARING, THAT WE GREET HEALTHY CONTROVERSY AS THE HALLMARK OF HEALTHY CHANGE."

"THE HOPES OF ALL MANKIND REST UPON US; NOT SIMPLY UPON THOSE OF US IN THIS CHAMBER, BUT UPON THE PEASANT IN LAOS, THE FISHERMAN IN NIGERIA, THE EXILE FROM CUBA, THE SPIRIT THAT MOVES EVERY MAN AND NATION WHO SHARES OUR HOPES FOR FREEDOM AND THE FUTURE."

On January 29, President Kennedy appeared before Congress to deliver his first State of the Union Message.

THE STATE OF THE UNION

State of the Union Message,
January 29, 1961

. . . It is a pleasure to return from whence I came. You are my oldest friends in Washington, and this House is my oldest home. It was here, more than fourteen years ago, that I first took the oath of Federal office. It was here, for fourteen years, that I gained both knowledge and inspiration from members of both parties in both Houses, from your wise and generous leaders, and from the pronouncements which I can vividly recall, sitting where you now sit, including the programs of two great Presidents, the undimmed eloquence of Churchill, the soaring idealism of Nehru, the steadfast words of General de Gaulle. To speak from this same historic rostrum is a sobering experience. To be back among so many friends is a happy one.

I am confident that that friendship will continue. Our Constitution wisely assigns both joint and separate roles to each branch of the government; and a President and a Congress who hold each other in mutual respect will neither permit nor attempt any trespass. For my part, I shall withhold from neither the Congress nor the people any fact or report, past, present or future, which is necessary for an informed judgment of our conduct and hazards. I shall neither shift the burden of executive decisions to the Congress, nor avoid responsibility for the outcome of those decisions.

I speak today in an hour of national peril and national opportunity. Before my term has ended, we shall have to test anew whether a nation organized and governed such as ours can endure. The outcome is by no means certain. The answers are by no means clear. All of us together—this Administration, this Congress, this nation—must forge those answers.

But today, were I to offer, after little more than a week in office, detailed legislation to remedy every national ill, the Congress would rightly wonder whether the desire for speed had replaced the duty of responsibility.

My remarks, therefore, will be limited. But they will also be candid. To state the facts frankly is not to despair the future nor indict the past. The prudent heir takes careful inventory of his legacies, and gives a faithful accounting to those whom he owes an obligation of trust. And, while the occasion does not call for another recital of our blessings and assets, we do have no greater asset than the willingness of a free and determined people, through its elected officials, to face all problems frankly and meet all dangers free from panic or fear.

I

The present state of our economy is disturbing. We take office in the wake of seven months of recession, three and one-half years of slack, seven years of diminished economic growth, and nine years of falling farm income.

Business bankruptcies have reached their highest level since the Great Depression. Since 1951 farm income has been squeezed down by 25 per cent. Save for a brief period in 1958, insured unemployment is at the highest peak in our history. Of some five and one-half million Americans who are without jobs, more than one million have been searching for work for more than four months. And during each month some 150,000 workers are exhausting their already meager jobless benefit rights.

Nearly one-eighth of those who are without jobs live almost without hope in nearly one hundred depressed and troubled areas. The rest include new school graduates unable to use their talents, farmers forced to give up their part-time jobs which helped balance their family budgets, skilled and unskilled workers laid off in such important industries as metals, machinery, automobiles and apparel.

Our recovery from the 1958 recession, moreover, was anemic and incomplete. Our Gross National Product never regained its full potential. Unemployment never returned to normal levels. Maximum use of our national industrial capacity was never restored.

In short, the American economy is in trouble. The most resourceful industrialized country on earth ranks among the last in the rate of economic growth. Since last spring our economic growth rate has actually receded. Business investment is in a decline. Profits have fallen below predicted levels. Construction is off. A million unsold automobiles are in inventory. Fewer people are working, and the average work week has shrunk well below forty hours. Yet prices have continued to rise, so that now too many Americans have *less* to spend for items that cost *more* to buy.

Economic prophecy is at best an uncertain art, as demonstrated by the prediction one year ago from this same podium that 1960 would be, and I quote, "the most prosperous year in our history." Nevertheless, forecasts of continued slack and only slightly reduced unemployment through 1961 and 1962 have been made with alarming unanimity, and this Administration does not intend to stand helplessly by.

We cannot afford to waste idle hours and empty plants while awaiting the end of the recession. We must show the world what a free economy can do, to reduce unemployment, to put unused capacity to work, to spur new productivity, and to foster higher economic growth within a range of sound fiscal policies and relative price stability.

I will propose to the Congress within the next fourteen days measures to improve unemployment compensation through temporary increases in duration on a self-supporting basis; to provide more food for the families of the unemployed, and to aid their needy children; to redevelop our areas of chronic labor surplus; to expand the services of the U.S. Employment Offices; to stimulate housing and construction; to secure more purchasing power for our lowest-paid workers by raising and expanding the minimum wage; to offer tax incentives for sound plant investment; to increase the development of natural resources; to encourage price stability; and to take other steps aimed at insuring a prompt recovery and paving the way for increased long-range growth. This is not a partisan program concentrating on our weaknesses; it is, I hope, a national program to realize our national strength.

II

Efficient expansion at home, stimulating the new plant and technology that can make our goods more competitive, is also the key to the international balance of payments problem. Laying aside all alarmist talk and panicky solutions, let us put that knotty problem in its proper perspective.

It is true that, since 1958, the gap between the dollars we spend or invest abroad and the dollars returned to us has substantially widened. This over-all deficit in our balance of payments increased by nearly $11 billion in the three years, and holders of dollars abroad converted them to gold in such a quantity as to cause a total outflow of nearly $5 billion of gold from our reserve. The 1959 deficit was caused in large part by the failure of our exports to penetrate foreign markets, the result both of restrictions on our goods and of our own uncompetitive prices. The 1960 deficit, on the other hand, was more the result of an increase in private capital outflow seeking new opportunity, higher return or speculative advantage abroad.

Meanwhile this country has continued to bear more than its share of the West's military and foreign aid obligations. Under existing policies, another deficit of $2 billion is predicted for 1961, and individuals in those countries whose dollar position once depended on these deficits for improvement now wonder aloud whether our gold reserves will remain sufficient to meet our own obligations.

All this is cause for concern, but it is not cause for panic. For our monetary and financial position remains exceedingly strong. Including our drawing rights in the International Monetary Fund and the gold reserve held as backing for our currency and Federal Reserve deposits, we have some $22 billion in total gold stocks and other international monetary reserves available, and I now pledge that their full strength stands behind the value of the dollar for use if needed.

Moreover, we hold large assets abroad—the total owed this nation far exceeds the claims upon our reserves—and our exports once again substantially exceed our imports.

In short, we need not, and we shall not, take any action to increase the dollar price of gold from $35 an ounce, to impose exchange controls, to reduce our antirecession efforts, to fall back on restrictive trade policies, or to weaken our commitments around the world.

This Administration will not distort the value of the dollar in any fashion. And this is a commitment.

Prudence and good sense do require, however, that new steps be taken to ease the payments deficit and prevent any gold crisis. Our success in world affairs has long depended in part upon foreign confidence in our ability to pay. A series of Executive Orders, legislative remedies and co-operative efforts with our allies will get under way immediately, aimed at attracting foreign investment and travel to this country, promoting American exports at stable prices and with more liberal government guarantees and financing, curbing tax and customs loopholes that encourage undue spending of private dollars abroad, and (through the Organization for Economic Co-operation and Development, the North Atlantic Treaty Organization and otherwise) sharing with our allies all efforts to provide for the common defense of the free world and the hopes for growth of the less-developed lands. While the current deficit lasts, ways will be found to ease our dollar outlays abroad without placing the full burden on the families of men whom we have asked to serve our flag overseas.

In short, whatever is required will be done to back up all our efforts abroad, and to make certain that, in the future as in the past, the dollar is as "sound as a dollar."

III

But more than our exchange of international payments is out of balance. The current Federal budget for fiscal 1961 is almost certain to show a net deficit. The budget already submitted for fiscal 1962 will remain in balance only if the Congress enacts all the revenue measures requested, and only if an earlier and sharper upturn in the economy than my economic advisers now think likely produces the tax revenues estimated. Nevertheless, a new Administration must of necessity build on the spending and revenue estimates already submitted. Within that framework, barring the development of urgent national defense needs or a worsening of the economy, it is my current intention to advocate a program of expenditures which, including revenues from a stimulation of the economy, will not of and by themselves unbalance the earlier budget.

However, we will do what must be done. For our national household is cluttered with unfinished and neglected tasks. Our cities are being engulfed in squalor. Twelve long years after Congress declared our goal to be "a decent home and a suitable environment for every American family," we still have 25 million Americans living in substandard homes. A new housing program under a new Housing and Urban Affairs Department will be needed this year.

Our classrooms contain two million more children than they can properly have room for, taught by ninety thousand teachers not properly qualified to teach. One-third of our most promising high school graduates are financially unable to continue the development of their talents. The war babies of the 1940's, who overcrowded our schools in the 1950's, are now descending in 1960 upon our colleges—with two college students for every one, ten years from now—and our colleges are ill prepared. We lack the scientists, the engineers and the teachers our world obligations require. We have neglected oceanography, saline water conversion and the basic research that lies at the root of all progress. Federal grants for both higher and public school education can no longer be delayed.

Medical research has achieved new wonders, but these wonders are too often beyond the reach of too many people, owing to a lack of income (particularly among the aged), a lack of hospital beds, a lack of nursing homes and a lack of doctors and dentists. Measures to provide health care for the aged under Social Security, and to increase the supply of both facilities and personnel, must be undertaken this year.

Our supply of clean water is dwindling. Organized and juvenile crimes cost the taxpayers millions of dollars each year, making it essential that we have improved enforcement and new legislative safeguards. The denial of constitutional rights to some of our fellow Americans on account of race, at the ballot box and elsewhere, disturbs the national conscience, and subjects us to the charge of world opinion that our democracy is not equal to the high promise of our heritage. Morality in private business has not been sufficiently spurred by morality in public business. A host of problems and projects in all fifty states, though not possible to include in this message, deserves, and will receive, the attention of both the Congress and the Executive Branch. On most of these matters, messages will be sent to the Congress within the next two weeks.

IV

But all these problems pale when placed beside those which confront us around the world. No man entering upon this office, regardless of his party, regardless of his previous service in Washington, could fail to be staggered upon learning, even in this brief ten-day period, the harsh enormity of the trials through which we must pass in the next four years. Each day the crises multiply. Each day their solution grows more difficult. Each day we draw nearer the hour of maximum danger, as weapons spread and hostile forces grow stronger. I feel I must inform the Congress that our analyses over the last ten days make it clear that, in each of the principal areas of crisis, the tide of events has been running out and time has not been our friend.

In Asia, the relentless pressures of the Chinese Communists menace the security of the entire area, from the borders of India and South Vietnam to the jungles of Laos, struggling to protect its newly won independence. We seek in Laos what we seek in all Asia, and, indeed, in all the world: freedom for the people and independence for the government. And this nation shall persevere in our pursuit of these objectives.

In Africa, the Congo has been brutally torn by civil strife, political unrest and public disorder. We shall continue to support the heroic efforts of the United Nations to restore peace and order, efforts which are now endangered by mounting tensions, unsolved problems and decreasing support from many member states.

In Latin America, Communist agents seeking to exploit that region's peaceful revolution of hope have established a base on Cuba, only ninety miles from our shores. Our difference with Cuba is not over the people's drive for a better life. Our objection is to their domination by foreign and domestic tyrannies. Cuban social and economic reform should be encouraged. Questions of economic and trade policy can always be negotiated, but Communist domination in this hemisphere can never be negotiated.

We are pledged to work with our sister republics to free the Americas of all such foreign domination and all tyranny, working toward the goal of a free hemisphere of free governments, extending from Cape Horn to the Arctic Circle.

In Europe our alliances are unfulfilled and in some disarray. The unity of NATO has been weakened by economic rivalry and partially eroded by national interest. It has not yet fully mobilized its resources nor fully achieved a common outlook. Yet no Altantic power can meet on its own the mutual problems now facing us in defense, foreign aid, monetary reserves and a host of other areas; and our close ties with those whose hopes and interests we share are among this nation's most powerful assets.

Our greatest challenge is still the world that lies beyond the Cold War, but the first great obstacle is still our relations with the Soviet Union and Communist China. We must never be lulled into believing that either power has yielded its ambitions for world domination, ambitions which they forcefully restated only a short time ago. On the contrary, our task is to convince them that aggression and subversion will not be profitable routes to pursue these ends. Open and peaceful competition—for prestige, for markets, for scientific achievement, even for men's minds—is something else again. For if Freedom and Communism were to compete for man's allegiance in a world of peace, I would look to the future with ever-increasing confidence.

To meet this array of challenges, to fulfill the role we cannot avoid on the world scene, we must re-examine and revise our whole arsenal of tools: military, economic and political.

One must not overshadow the other. On the Presidential coat of arms, the American eagle holds in his right talon the olive branch, while in his left he holds a bundle of arrows. We intend to give equal attention to both.

First, we must strengthen our military tools. We are moving into a period of uncertain risk and great commitment in which both the military and diplomatic possibilities require a free world force so powerful as to make any aggression clearly futile. Yet in the past, lack of a consistent, coherent military strategy, the absence of basic assumptions about our national requirements and the faulty estimates and duplications arising from interservice rivalries have all made it difficult to assess accurately how adequate, or inadequate, our defenses really are.

I have, therefore, instructed the Secretary of Defense to reappraise our entire defense strategy: our ability to fulfill our commitments; the effectiveness, vulnerability and dispersal of our strategic bases, forces and warning systems; the efficiency and economy of our operation and organization; the elimination of obsolete bases and installations; and the adequacy, modernization and mobility of our present conventional and nuclear forces and weapons systems in the light of present and future dangers. I have asked for preliminary conclusions by the end of February, and I then shall recommend whatever legislative, budgetary or executive action is needed in the light of these conclusions.

In the meantime, I have asked the Defense Secretary to initiate immediately three new steps most clearly needed now:

1. I have directed prompt action to increase our airlift capacity. Obtaining additional air transport mobility, and obtaining it now, will better assure the ability of our conventional forces to respond, with discrimination and speed, to any prob-

lem at any spot on the globe at any moment's notice. In particular it will enable us to meet any deliberate effort to avoid or divert our forces by starting limited wars in widely scattered parts of the world.

2. I have directed prompt action to step up our Polaris submarine program. Using unobligated shipbuilding funds now (to let contracts originally scheduled for the next fiscal year) will build and place on station, at least nine months earlier than planned, substantially more units of a crucial deterrent, a fleet that will never attack first, but will possess sufficient powers of retaliation, concealed beneath the seas, to discourage any aggressor from launching an attack upon our security.

3. I have directed prompt action to accelerate our entire missile program. Until the Secretary of Defense's reappraisal is completed, the emphasis here will be largely on improved organization and decision-making, on cutting down the wasteful duplications and the time-lag that have handicapped our whole family of missiles. If we are to keep the peace, we need an invulnerable missile force powerful enough to deter any aggressor from even threatening an attack that he would know could not destroy enough of our force to prevent his own destruction. For as I said upon taking the oath of office: "Only when our arms are sufficient beyond doubt can we be certain beyond doubt that they will never be employed."

Second, we must improve our economic tools. Our role is essential and unavoidable in the construction of a sound and expanding economy for the entire non-Communist world, helping other nations build the strength to meet their own problems, to satisfy their own aspirations, to surmount their own dangers. The problems in achieving this goal are towering and unprecedented. The response must be towering and unprecedented as well, much as Lend-Lease and the Marshall Plan, which brought such fruitful results, were in earlier years.

I intend to ask the Congress for authority to establish a new and more effective program for assisting the economic, educational and social development of other countries and continents. That program must stimulate and take more effectively into account the contributions of our allies, and provide central policy direction for all our own programs that now so often overlap, conflict or diffuse our energies and resources. Such a program, compared to past programs, will require: more flexibility for short-run emergencies; more commitment to long-term development; new attention to education at all levels; greater emphasis on the recipient nations' role, their effort, their purpose, with greater social justice for their people, broader distribution and participation by their people and more efficient public administration and more efficient tax systems of their own; and orderly planning for national and regional development instead of a piecemeal approach.

I hope the Senate will take early action approving the Convention establishing the Organization for Economic Co-operation and Development. This will be an important instrument in sharing with our allies this development effort, working toward the time when each nation will contribute in proportion to its ability to pay. For, while we are prepared to assume our full share of these huge burdens, we cannot and must not be expected to bear them alone.

To our sister republics to the south, we have pledged a new Alliance for Progress—*Alianza para Progreso*. Our goal is a free and prosperous Latin America, realizing for all its states and all its citizens a degree of economic and social progress that matches their historic contributions of culture, intellect and liberty. To start this nation's role at this time in that alliance of neighbors, I am recommending the following:

1. That the Congress appropriate in full the $500 million fund pledged by the Act of Bogotá, to be used not as an instrument of the Cold War, but as a first step in the sound development of the Americas.

2. That a new Inter-Departmental Task Force be established under the leadership of the Department of State, to co-ordinate at the highest level all policies and programs of concern to the Americas.

3. That our delegates to the Organization of American States, working with those of other members, strengthen that body as an instrument to preserve the peace and to prevent foreign domination anywhere in the hemisphere.

4. That, in co-operation with other nations, we launch a new hemispheric attack on illiteracy and inadequate educational opportunities at all levels; and finally,

5. That a Food-for-Peace mission be sent immediately to Latin America to explore ways in which our vast food abundance can be used to help end hunger and malnutrition in certain areas of suffering in our own hemisphere.

This Administration is expanding its Food-for-Peace Program in every possible way. The product of our abundance must be used more effectively to relieve hunger and help economic growth in all corners of the globe. And I have asked the director of this program to recommend additional ways in which these surpluses can advance the interests of world peace, including the establishment of world food reserves.

An even more valuable national asset is our reservoir of dedicated men and women, not only on our college campuses but in every age group, who have indicated their desire to contribute their skills, their efforts and a part of their lives to the fight for world order. We can mobilize this talent through the formation of a National Peace Corps, enlisting the services of all those with the desire and capacity to help foreign lands meet their urgent needs for trained personnel.

Finally, while our attention is centered on the development of the non-Communist world, we must never forget our hopes for the ultimate freedom and welfare of the Eastern European peoples. In order to be prepared to help re-establish historic ties of friendship, I am asking the Congress for increased discretion to use economic tools in this area whenever this is found to be clearly in the national interest. This will require amendment to the Mutual Defense Assistance Control Act along the lines I proposed as a member of the Senate, and upon which the Senate voted last summer. Meanwhile, I hope to explore with the Polish Government the possibility of using our frozen Polish funds on projects of peace that will demonstrate our abiding friendship for and interest in the people of Poland.

Third, we must sharpen our political and diplomatic tools— the means of co-operation and agreement on which an enforceable world order must ultimately rest.

I have already taken steps to co-ordinate and expand our disarmament effort, to increase our programs of research and study, and to make arms control a central goal of our national policy under my direction. The deadly arms race, and the huge resources it absorbs, have too long overshadowed all else we must do. We must prevent that arms race from spreading to new nations, to new nuclear powers and to the reaches of outer space. We must make certain that our negotiators are better informed and better prepared to formulate workable proposals of our own and to make sound judgments about the proposals of others.

I have asked the other governments concerned to agree to a reasonable delay in the talks on a nuclear test ban; and it is our intention to resume negotiations prepared to reach a final agreement with any nation that is equally willing to agree to an effective and enforceable treaty.

We must increase our support of the United Nations as an instrument to end the Cold War instead of an arena in which to fight it. In recognition of its increasing importance and the doubling of its membership: we are enlarging and strengthening our own mission to the UN; we shall help insure that it is properly financed; we shall work to see that the integrity of the office of the Secretary General is maintained.

And I would address a special plea to the smaller nations of the world to join with us in strengthening this organization, which is far more essential to their security than it is to ours, the only body in the world where no nation need be powerful to be secure, where every nation has an equal voice, and where any nation can exert influence not according to the strength of its armies but according to the strength of its ideas. It deserves the support of all.

Finally, this Administration intends to explore promptly all possible areas of co-operation with the Soviet Union and other nations "to invoke the wonders of science instead of its terrors." Specifically, I now invite all nations, including the Soviet Union, to join with us in developing a weather prediction program, in a new communication satellite program and in preparation for probing the distant planets of Mars and Venus, probes which may someday unlock the deepest secrets of the universe.

Today this country is ahead in the science and technology of space, while the Soviet Union is ahead in the capacity to lift large vehicles into orbit. Both nations would help themselves as well as other nations by removing these endeavors from the bitter and wasteful competition of the Cold War. The United States would be willing to join with the Soviet Union and the scientists of all nations in a greater effort to make the fruits of this new knowledge available to all, and, beyond that, in an effort to extend farm technology to hungry nations, to wipe out disease, to increase the exchanges of scientists and their knowledge, and to make our own laboratories available to technicians of other lands who lack the facilities to pursue their own work. Where nature makes natural allies of us all, we can demonstrate that beneficial relations are possible even with those with whom we most deeply disagree, and this must someday be the basis of world peace and world law.

V

I have commented on the state of the domestic economy, our balance of payments, our Federal and social budget and the state of the world. I would like to conclude with a few remarks about the state of the Executive Branch. We have found it full of honest and useful public servants, but their capacity to act decisively at the exact time action is needed has too often been muffled in the morass of committees, timidities and fictitious theories which have created a growing gap between decision and execution, between planning and reality. In a time of rapidly deteriorating situations at home and abroad, this is bad for the public service and particularly bad for the country; and we mean to make a change.

I have pledged myself and my colleagues in the Cabinet to a continuous encouragement of initiative, responsibility and energy in serving the public interest. Let every public servant know, whether his post is high or low, that a man's rank and reputation in this Administration will be determined by the size of the job he does, and not by the size of his staff, his office or his budget. Let it be clear that this Administration recognizes the value of dissent and daring, that we greet healthy controversy as the hallmark of healthy change. Let the public service be a proud and lively career. And let every man and woman who works in any area of our national government, in any branch, at any level, be able to say with pride and with honor in future years: "I served the United States Government in that hour of our nation's need."

For only with complete dedication by us all to the national interest can we bring our country through the troubled years that lie ahead. Our problems are critical. The tide is unfavorable. The news will be worse before it is better. And while hoping and working for the best, we should prepare ourselves now for the worst.

We cannot escape our dangers; neither must we let them drive us into panic or narrow isolation. In many areas of the world where the balance of power already rests with our adversaries, the forces of freedom are sharply divided. It is one of the ironies of our time that the techniques of a harsh and repressive system should be able to instill discipline and ardor in its servants, while the blessings of liberty have too often stood for privilege, materialism and a life of ease.

But I have a different view of liberty.

Life in 1961 will not be easy. Wishing it, predicting it, even asking for it, will not make it so. There will be further setbacks before the tide is turned. But turn it we must. The hopes of all mankind rest upon us; not simply upon those of us in this chamber, but upon the peasant in Laos, the fisherman in Nigeria, the exile from Cuba, the spirit that moves every man and nation who shares our hopes for freedom and the future. And in the final analysis, they rest most of all upon the pride and perseverance of our fellow citizens of the great Republic.

In the words of a great President, whose birthday we honor today, closing his final State of the Union Message sixteen years ago, "We pray that we may be worthy of the unlimited opportunities that God has given us."

CHAPTER III
EARLY CRISES

. . . "IF THE SELF-DISCIPLINE OF THE FREE CANNOT MATCH THE
IRON DISCIPLINE OF THE MAILED FIST, IN ECONOMIC, POLITICAL,
SCIENTIFIC AND ALL THE OTHER KINDS OF STRUGGLES AS WELL AS
THE MILITARY, THEN THE PERIL TO FREEDOM WILL CONTINUE
TO RISE."

"THE COMPLACENT, THE SELF-INDULGENT, THE SOFT SOCIETIES
ARE ABOUT TO BE SWEPT AWAY WITH THE DEBRIS OF HISTORY."

"WE ARE NOT AGAINST ANY MAN, OR ANY NATION, OR ANY SYSTEM,
EXCEPT AS IT IS HOSTILE TO FREEDOM."

". . . OUR PATIENCE AT THE BARGAINING TABLE IS NEARLY INEX-
HAUSTIBLE, THOUGH OUR CREDULITY IS LIMITED. . . ."

When a reporter asked President Kennedy why, in his In-augural Address, he had limited himself to discussing Amer-ica's position in the world, the President replied simply that what was involved was the issue of war and peace and the sur-vival of our system, perhaps of the planet itself, and that this must necessarily be of primary concern to all of us.

Events soon justified his preoccupation with the inter-national scene. In the early months of his Administration, there were crises of major dimensions in Laos, Cuba and the Congo.

At the time the new Administration took office, affairs in the Congo had deteriorated nearly to the point of chaos, and there was increasingly ominous evidence of Soviet interven-tion. In a press conference on February 15, the President issued a pointed warning.

THE CONGO

I am . . . seriously concerned at what appears to be a threat of unilateral intervention in the internal affairs of the Republic of the Congo. I find it difficult to believe that any government is really planning to take so dangerous and irresponsible a step.

. . . I feel it important that there should be no misunderstanding of the position of the United States in such an eventuality. The United States has supported and will continue to support the United Nations' presence in the Congo. The United States considers that the only legal authority entitled to speak for the Congo as a whole is a government established under the Chief of State, President Kasavubu, who has been seated in the General Assembly of the United Nations by a majority vote of its members. The broadening of the government under President Kasavubu is a quite legitimate subject of discussion, and such discussions have been going on in Léopoldville and in New York, but the purported recognition of Congolese factions as so-called governments in other parts of that divided country can only confuse and make more difficult the task of securing Congolese independence and unity.

The United Nations offers the best, if not the only, possibility for the restoration of conditions of stability and order in the Congo.

The press reports this afternoon that Prime Minister Nehru has stated, and I quote, "If the United Nations goes out of the Congo, it will be a disaster." I strongly agree with this view. Only by the presence of the United Nations in the Congo can peace be kept in Africa. I would conceive it to be the duty of the United States, and indeed of all members of the United Nations, to defend the Charter of the United Nations by opposing any attempt by any government to intervene unilaterally in the Congo.

LAOS

In a press conference on March 23 the President turned his attention to Laos.

Eighth Press Conference,
March 23, 1961

I want to talk about Laos. It is important, I think, for all Americans to understand this difficult and potentially dangerous problem. In my last conversation with General Eisenhower, the day before the Inauguration, we spent more time on this hard matter than on any other one thing. And since then it has been steadily before the Administration as the most immediate of the problems we found on taking office.

Our special concern with the problem in Laos goes back to 1954. That year, at Geneva, a large group of powers agreed to a settlement of the struggle for Indo-China. Laos was one of the new states which had recently emerged from the French

Union, and it was the clear promise of the 1954 settlement that this new country would be neutral, free of external domination by anyone. The new country contained contending factions, but in its first years real progress was made toward a unified and neutral status. But the efforts of a Communist-dominated group to destroy this neutrality never ceased, and in the last half of 1960 a series of sudden maneuvers occurred, and the Communists and their supporters turned to a new and greatly intensified military effort. . . .

In this military advance the local Communist forces, known as the Pathet Lao, have had increasing support and direction from outside. Soviet planes, I regret to say, have been conspicuous in a large-scale airlift into the battle area—over one thousand sorties since December 13, 1960—and a whole supporting set of combat specialists, mainly from Communist North Vietnam, and heavier weapons have been provided from outside, all with the clear object of destroying by military action the agreed neutrality of Laos. It is this new dimension of externally supported warfare that creates the present grave problem.

The position of this Administration has been carefully considered, and we have sought to make it just as clear as we know how to the governments concerned. First: we strongly and unreservedly support the goal of a neutral and independent Laos, tied to no outside power or group of powers, threatening no one, and free from any domination. Our support for the present duly constituted government is aimed entirely and exclusively at that result, and if in the past there has been any possible ground for misunderstanding of our support for a truly neutral Laos, there should be none now.

Second, if there is to be a peaceful solution, there must be

a cessation of the present armed attacks by externally supported Communists. If these attacks do not stop, those who
support a genuinely neutral Laos will have to consider their
response. The shape of this necessary response will of course
be carefully considered not only here in Washington but in
the SEATO conference with our allies which begins next Monday. SEATO—the Southeast Asia Treaty Organization—was
organized in 1954 with strong leadership from our last Administration, and all members of SEATO have undertaken
special treaty responsibilities toward an aggression against
Laos.

No one should doubt our own resolution on this point. We
are faced with a clear threat of a change in the internationally
agreed position of Laos. This threat runs counter to the will
of the Laotian people, who wish only to be independent and
neutral. It is posed rather by the military operations of internal dissident elements directed from outside the country. This
is what must end if peace is to be kept in Southeast Asia.

Third, we are earnestly in favor of constructive negotiation,
among the nations concerned and among the leaders of Laos,
which can help Laos back to the pathway of independence
and genuine neutrality. We strongly support the present British
proposal of a prompt end of hostilities and prompt negotiation. We are always conscious of the obligation which rests
upon all members of the United Nations to seek peaceful solutions to problems of this sort. We hope that others may be
equally aware of this responsibility.

My fellow Americans, Laos is far away from America, but
the world is small. Its two million peaceful people live in a
country three times the size of Austria. The security of all of
Southeast Asia will be endangered if Laos loses its neutral in-

dependence. Its own safety runs with the safety of us all, in real neutrality observed by all.

I want to make it clear to the American people, and to all the world, that all we want in Laos is peace, not war; a truly neutral government, not a Cold War pawn; a settlement concluded at the conference table, not on the battlefield. Our response will be in close co-operation with our allies and the wishes of the Laotian Government. We will not be provoked, trapped or drawn into this or any other situation. But I know that every American would want to be aware that his obligations to the people and security of the free world and ourselves may be achieved.

CUBA

During 1960 the government and the people of the United States had followed events in Cuba with growing apprehension. In a press conference on January 25, 1961 President Kennedy touched on the subject.

First Press Conference,
January 25, 1961

QUESTION: Under what conditions would you consider reopening diplomatic relations with Cuba, and are you considering such a step now?

THE PRESIDENT: Well, to take the last part first, we are

not considering such a step at the present time. . . . This Administration is extremely interested in movements in Latin America and Central America, and the Caribbean, which provide a better life for the people. . . . What we are, of course, concerned about is when these movements are seized by external forces and directed not to the improving of the welfare of the people involved, but toward imposing an ideology which is alien to this hemisphere. That is a matter of concern, particularly when that intervention takes the form of military support which threatens the security and peace of the Western Hemisphere.

In a press conference on April 12 the subject of Cuba came up again.

Ninth Press Conference,
April 12, 1961

QUESTION: Mr. President, your white paper last year—last week—referred in very diplomatic language to the takeover by Communism in Cuba. Is it your view that Fidel Castro is personally a Communist?

THE PRESIDENT: Well, he has indicated his admiration on many occasions for the Communist revolution. He has appointed a great many Communists to high positions. . . . I would not want to characterize Mr. Castro, except to say that by his own words he has indicated his hostility to democratic rule in this hemisphere, to democratic liberal leaders in many of the countries of the hemisphere who are attempting to improve the life of their people, and has associated himself most

intimately with the Sino-Soviet bloc, and has indicated his desire to spread the influence of that bloc throughout this hemisphere.

*Then before dawn on the morning of April 17 a military
force of Cuban exiles attempted to invade their homeland,
and suffered a disastrous defeat. Under Mr. Kennedy, as well
as earlier under Mr. Eisenhower, the United States Government had given various forms of assistance to the exiles, and
the defeat was a heavy blow. It was perhaps the most painful
incident in the first year of President Kennedy's Administration.*

*Three days after the event the President dealt with the
subject in a speech to the American Society of Newspaper
Editors.*

*Address to the American Society of Newspaper Editors,
April 20, 1961*

The President of a great democracy such as ours, and the
editors of great newspapers such as yours, owe a common
obligation to the people: an obligation to present the facts,
to present them with candor, and to present them in perspective. It is with that obligation in mind that I have decided in
the last twenty-four hours to discuss briefly at this time the
recent events in Cuba.

On that unhappy island, as in so many other arenas of the
contest for freedom, the news has grown worse instead of
better. I have emphasized before that this was a struggle of
Cuban patriots against a Cuban dictator. While we could not
be expected to hide our sympathies, we made it repeatedly

clear that the armed forces of this country would not intervene in any way.

Any unilateral American intervention, in the absence of an
external attack upon ourselves or an ally, would have been
contrary to our traditions and to our international obligations.
But let the record show that our restraint is not inexhaustible.
Should it ever appear that the inter-American doctrine of non-
interference merely conceals or excuses a policy of nonaction,
if the nations of this hemisphere should fail to meet their commitments against outside Communist penetration, then I want
it clearly understood that this government will not hesitate in
meeting its primary obligations which are to the security of our
nation.

Should that time ever come, we do not intend to be lectured
on "intervention" by those whose character was stamped for
all time on the bloody streets of Budapest. Nor would we
expect or accept the same outcome which this small band of
gallant Cuban refugees must have known that they were chanc-
ing, determined as they were against heavy odds to pursue
their courageous attempts to regain their island's freedom.

But Cuba is not an island unto itself; and our concern is
not ended by mere expressions of nonintervention or regret.
This is not the first time in either ancient or recent history
that a small band of freedom fighters has engaged the armor
of totalitarianism.

It is not the first time that Communist tanks have rolled
over gallant men and women fighting to redeem the independence of their homeland. Nor is it by any means the final episode in the eternal struggle of liberty against tyranny, anywhere
on the face of the globe, including Cuba itself.

Mr. Castro has said that these were mercenaries. According to press reports, the final message to be relayed from the refugee forces on the beach came from the rebel commander when asked if he wished to be evacuated. His answer was: "I will never leave this country." That is not the reply of a mercenary. He has gone now to join in the mountains countless other guerrilla fighters, who are equally determined that the dedication of those who gave their lives shall not be forgotten, and that Cuba must not be abandoned to the Communists. And we do not intend to abandon it either.

The Cuban people have not yet spoken their final piece. . . . Meanwhile we will not accept Mr. Castro's attempts to blame this nation for the hatred with which his onetime supporters now regard his repression. But there are from this sobering episode useful lessons for all to learn. Some may be still obscure, and await further information. Some are clear today.

First, it is clear that the forces of Communism are not to be underestimated, in Cuba or anywhere else in the world. The advantages of a police state, its use of mass terror and arrests to prevent the spread of free dissent, cannot be overlooked by those who expect the fall of every fanatic tyrant. If the self-discipline of the free cannot match the iron discipline of the mailed fist, in economic, political, scientific and all the other kinds of struggles as well as the military, then the peril to freedom will continue to rise.

Second, it is clear that this nation, in concert with all the free nations of this hemisphere, must take an even closer and more realistic look at the menace of external Communist intervention and domination in Cuba. The American people are not complacent about Iron Curtain tanks and planes less than ninety miles from our shores. But a nation of Cuba's size is less a threat to our survival than it is a base for subverting the survival of other free nations throughout the hemisphere. It is not primarily our interest or our security but theirs which is now, today, in the greater peril. It is for their sake as well as our own that we must show our will.

The evidence is clear, and the hour is late. We and our Latin friends will have to face the fact that we cannot postpone any longer the real issue of the survival of freedom in this hemisphere itself. On that issue, unlike perhaps some others, there can be no middle ground. Together we must build a hemisphere where freedom can flourish; and where any free nation under outside attack of any kind can be assured that all of our resources stand ready to respond to any request for assistance.

Third, and finally, it is clearer than ever that we face a relentless struggle in every corner of the globe that goes far beyond the clash of armies or even nuclear armaments. The armies are there, and in large number. The nuclear armaments are there. But they serve primarily as the shield behind which subversion, infiltration and a host of other tactics steadily advance, picking off vulnerable areas one by one in situations which do not permit our own armed intervention.

Power is the hallmark of this offensive—power and discipline and deceit. The legitimate discontent of yearning peoples is exploited. The legitimate trappings of self-determination are employed. But once in power, all talk of discontent is repressed, all self-determination disappears, and the promise of a revolution of hope is betrayed, as in Cuba, into a reign of terror. Those who staged automatic "riots" in the streets of free nations over the effort of a small group of young Cubans to regain their freedom should recall the long roll call of refugees who cannot now go back—to Hungary, to North Korea, to

North Vietnam, to East Germany or to Poland, or to any of the other lands from which a steady stream of refugees pours forth, in eloquent testimony to the cruel oppression now holding sway in their homelands.

We dare not fail to see the insidious nature of this new and deeper struggle. We dare not fail to grasp the new concepts, the new tools, the new sense of urgency we will need to combat it, whether in Cuba or South Vietnam. And we dare not fail to realize that this struggle is taking place every day, without fanfare, in thousands of villages and markets, day and night, and in classrooms all over the globe.

The message of Cuba, of Laos, of the rising din of Communist voices in Asia and Latin America—these messages are all the same. The complacent, the self-indulgent, the soft societies are about to be swept away with the debris of history. Only the strong, only the industrious, only the determined, only the courageous, only the visionary who determine the real nature of our struggle can possibly survive.

No greater task faces this nation or this Administration. No other challenge is more deserving of our every effort and energy. Too long we have fixed our eyes on traditional military needs, on armies prepared to cross borders or missiles poised for flight. Now it should be clear that this is no longer enough, that our security may be lost piece by piece, country by country, without the firing of a single missile or the crossing of a single border.

We intend to profit from this lesson. We intend to re-examine and reorient our forces of all kinds, our tactics and other institutions here in this community. We intend to intensify our efforts for a struggle in many ways more difficult than war, where disappointment will often accompany us.

For I am convinced that we in this country and in the free world possess the necessary resources, and all the skill, and the added strength that comes from a belief in the freedom of man. And I am equally convinced that history will record the fact that this bitter struggle reached its climax in the late 1950's and early 1960's. Let me then make clear as the President of the United States that I am determined upon our system's survival and success, regardless of the cost and regardless of the peril.

NATURE OF THE CONFLICT

The grave events on the international scene—always changing but in their implications always the same—offered President Kennedy many opportunities to state his views on the nature of the conflict. In his second State of the Union Message he dealt with the subject at length. Following are excerpts from that important message:

Special Message to the Congress on Urgent National Needs, May 25, 1961

. . . The Constitution imposes upon me the obligation to "from time to time give to the Congress information of the State of the Union." While this has traditionally been interpreted as an annual affair, this tradition has been broken in extraordinary times.

These are extraordinary times. And we face an extraordinary challenge. Our strength as well as our convictions have imposed upon this nation the role of leader in freedom's cause.

No role in history could be more difficult or more important. We stand for freedom. That is our conviction for ourselves; that is our only commitment to others. No friend, no neutral and no adversary should think otherwise. We are not against any man, or any nation, or any system, except as it is hostile to freedom. Nor am I here to present a new military doctrine, bearing any one name or aimed at any one area. I am here to promote the freedom doctrine.

The great battleground for the defense and expansion of freedom today is . . . Asia, Latin America, Africa and the Middle East, the lands of the rising peoples. Their revolution is the greatest in human history. They seek an end to injustice, tyranny and exploitation. More than an end, they seek a beginning.

And theirs is a revolution which we would support regardless of the Cold War, and regardless of which political or economic route they should choose to freedom.

For the adversaries of freedom did not create the revolution; nor did they create the conditions which compel it. But they are seeking to ride the crest of its wave, to capture it for themselves.

Yet their aggression is more often concealed than open. They have fired no missiles, and their troops are seldom seen. They send arms, agitators, aid, technicians and propaganda to every troubled area. But where fighting is required, it is usually done by others, by guerrillas striking at night, by assassins striking alone—assassins who have taken the lives of four thousand civil officers in the last twelve months in Vietnam alone—by subversives and saboteurs and insurrectionists, who in some cases control whole areas inside of independent nations.

With these formidable weapons, the adversaries of freedom plan to consolidate their territory, to exploit, to control, and finally to destroy the hopes of the world's newest nations; and they have ambitions to do it before the end of this decade. It is a contest of will and purpose as well as force and violence, a battle for minds and souls as well as lives and territory. And in that contest, we cannot stand aside.

We stand, as we have always stood from our earliest beginnings, for the independence and equality of nations. This nation was born of revolution and raised in freedom. And we do not intend to leave an open road for despotism.

There is no single simple policy which meets this challenge. Experience has taught us that no one nation has the power or the wisdom to solve all the problems of the world or manage its revolutionary tides; that extending our commitments does not always increase our security; that any initiative carries with it the risk of a temporary defeat; that nuclear weapons cannot prevent subversion; that no free peoples can be kept free without will and energy of their own; and that no two nations or situations are exactly alike. . . .

We are determined, as a nation in 1961, that freedom shall survive and succeed; and whatever the peril and setbacks, we have some very large advantages.

The first is the simple fact that we are on the side of liberty, and since the beginning of history, and particularly since the end of the Second World War, liberty has been winning out all over the globe.

A second great asset is that we are not alone. We have

friends and allies all over the world who share our devotion to freedom. May I cite as a symbol of traditional and effective friendship the great ally I am about to visit—France. I look forward to my visit to France, and to my discussion with a great captain of the Western world, President de Gaulle, as a meeting of particular significance, permitting the kind of close and ranging consultation that will strengthen both our countries and serve the common purposes of world-wide peace and liberty. Such serious conversations do not require a pale unanimity; they are rather the instruments of trust and understanding over a long road.

A third asset is our desire for peace. It is sincere, and I believe the world knows it. We are proving it in our patience at the test ban table, and we are proving it in the UN, where our efforts have been directed to maintaining that organization's usefulness as a protector of the independence of small nations. In these and other instances, the response of our opponents has not been encouraging.

Yet it is important that they should know that our patience at the bargaining table is nearly inexhaustible, though our credulity is limited; that our hopes for peace are unfailing, while our determination to protect our security is resolute. For these reasons I have long thought it wise to meet with the Soviet Premier for a personal exchange of views. A meeting in Vienna turned out to be convenient for us both; and the Austrian Government has kindly made us welcome. No formal agenda is planned and no negotiation will be undertaken; but we will make clear that America's enduring concern is for both peace *and* freedom; that we are anxious to live in harmony with the Russian people; that we seek no conquests, no satellites, no riches; that we seek only the day when "nation shall not lift up sword against nation, neither shall they learn war any more."

Finally, our greatest asset in this struggle is the American people—their willingness to pay the price for these programs; to understand and accept a long struggle; to share their resources with other, less fortunate peoples; to meet the tax levels and close the tax loopholes I have requested; to exercise self-restraint instead of pushing up wages or prices, or over-producing certain crops, or spreading military secrets, or urging unessential expenditures or improper monopolies or harmful work stoppages; to serve in the Peace Corps or the Armed Services or the Federal Civil Service or the Congress; to strive for excellence in their schools, in their cities and in their physical fitness and that of their children; to take part in Civil Defense; to pay higher postal rates, and higher pay-roll taxes and higher teachers' salaries, in order to strengthen our society; to show friendship to students and visitors from other lands who visit us and go back in many cases to be the future leaders, with an image of America—and I want that image, and I know you do, to be affirmative and positive—and, finally, to practice democracy at home, in all states, with all races, to respect each other and to protect the constitutional rights of all citizens.

I have not asked for a single program which did not cause one or all Americans some inconvenience, or some hardship, or some sacrifice. But they have responded; and you in the Congress have responded to your duty, and I feel confident in asking today for a similar response to these new and larger demands. . . .

CHAPTER IV
DEFENSE

"THE PRIMARY PURPOSE OF OUR ARMS IS PEACE, NOT WAR . . ."

"THE BASIC PROBLEMS FACING THE WORLD TODAY ARE NOT SUS-
CEPTIBLE TO A MILITARY SOLUTION."

"OUR ARMS WILL NEVER BE USED TO STRIKE THE FIRST BLOW IN
ANY ATTACK."

"WE DARE NOT TEMPT THEM WITH WEAKNESS. FOR ONLY WHEN
OUR ARMS ARE SUFFICIENT BEYOND DOUBT CAN WE BE CERTAIN
BEYOND DOUBT THAT THEY WILL NEVER BE EMPLOYED."

"ANY POTENTIAL AGGRESSOR CONTEMPLATING AN ATTACK ON ANY
PART OF THE FREE WORLD WITH ANY KIND OF WEAPONS, CON-
VENTIONAL OR NUCLEAR, MUST KNOW THAT OUR RESPONSE WILL
BE SUITABLE, SELECTIVE, SWIFT AND EFFECTIVE."

In a year of nerve-racking international tensions, there was bound to be deep preoccupation with matters of national security. In this area as in others the new Administration brought fresh appraisals of old problems, and—inevitably— significant new emphases.

The President's first major statement on national security came on March 28 in his special message to the Congress on the defense budget.

BASIC DEFENSE POLICIES

Special Message to the Congress on the Defense Budget, March 28, 1961

In my role as Commander-in-Chief of the American Armed Forces, and with my concern over the security of this nation now and in the future, no single question of policy has concerned me more since entering upon these responsibilities than the adequacy of our present and planned military forces to accomplish our major national security objectives. . . .

1. The primary purpose of our arms is peace, not war: to make certain that they will never have to be used; to deter all wars, general or limited, nuclear or conventional, large or small; to convince all potential aggressors that any attack would be futile; to provide backing for diplomatic settlement of disputes; to insure the adequacy of our bargaining power for an end to the arms race. The basic problems facing the world today are not susceptible to a military solution. Neither our strategy nor our psychology as a nation, and certainly not our economy, must become dependent upon the permanent maintenance of a large military establishment. Our military posture must be sufficiently flexible and under control to be consistent with our efforts to explore all possibilities and to take every step to lessen tensions, to obtain peaceful solutions and to secure arms limitations. Diplomacy and defense are no longer distinct alternatives, one to be used where the other fails; each must complement the other.

Disarmament, so difficult and so urgent, has been much discussed since 1945, but progress has not been made. Recrimination in such matters is seldom useful, and we for our part are determined to try again. In so doing, we note that, in the public position of both sides in recent years, the determination to be strong has been coupled with announced willingness to negotiate. For our part, we know there can be dialectical truth in such a position, and we shall do all we can to prove it in action. This budget is wholly consistent with our earnest desire for serious conversation with the other side on disarmament. If genuine progress is made, then as tension is reduced, so will be our arms.

2. Our arms will never be used to strike the first blow in any attack. This is not a confession of weakness but a statement of strength. It is our national tradition. We must offset whatever advantage this may appear to hand an aggressor by so increasing the capability of our forces to respond swiftly and effectively to any aggressive move as to convince any would-be aggressor that such a movement would be too futile and costly to undertake. In the area of general war, this doctrine means that such capability must rest with that portion of our forces which would survive the initial attack. We are not creating forces for a first strike against any other nation. We shall never threaten, provoke or initiate aggression; but if aggression should come, our response will be swift and effective.

3. Our arms must be adequate to meet our commitments and insure our security, without being bound by arbitrary budget ceilings. This nation can afford to be strong; it cannot afford to be weak. We shall do what is needed to make and to keep us strong. We must, of course, take advantage of every opportunity to reduce military outlays as a result of scientific or managerial progress, new strategic concepts, a more

efficient, manageable and thus more effective defense establishment, or international agreements for the control and limitation of arms. But we must not shrink from additional costs where they are necessary. The additional $650 million in expenditures for fiscal 1962 which I am recommending today, while relatively small, is too urgent to be governed by a budget largely decided before our defense review had been completed. Indeed, in the long run the net effect of all the changes I am recommending will be to provide a more economical budget. But I cannot promise that in later years we need not be prepared to spend still more for what is indispensable. Much depends on the course followed by other nations. As a proportion of Gross National Product, as a share of our total budget, and in comparison with our national effort in earlier times of war, this increase in defense expenditures is still substantially below what our citizens have been willing and are now able to support as insurance on their security—insurance we hope is never needed, but insurance we must nevertheless purchase.

4. Our arms must be subject to ultimate civilian control and command at all times, in war as well as peace. The basic decisions on our participation in any conflict and our response to any threat, including all decisions relating to the use of nuclear weapons, or the escalation of a small war into a large one, will be made by the regularly constituted civilian authorities. This requires effective and protected organization, procedures, facilities and communication in the event of attack directed toward this objective, as well as defensive measures designed to insure thoughtful and selective decisions by the civilian authorities. This message and budget also reflect that basic principle. The Secretary of Defense and I have had the

earnest counsel of our senior military advisers and many others, and in fact they support the great majority of the decisions reflected in this budget. But I have not delegated to anyone else the responsibilities for decision which are imposed upon me by the Constitution.

5. Our strategic arms and defenses must be adequate to deter any deliberate nuclear attack on the United States or our allies by making clear to any potential aggressor that sufficient retaliatory forces will be able to survive a first strike and penetrate his defenses in order to inflict unacceptable losses upon him. As I indicated in an address to the Senate some thirty-one months ago, this deterrence does not depend upon a simple comparison of missiles on hand before an attack. It has been publicly acknowledged for several years that this nation has not led the world in missile strength. Moreover, we will not strike first in any conflict. But what we have, and must continue to have, is the ability to survive a first blow and respond with devastating power. This deterrent power depends not only on the number of our missiles and bombers, but on their state of readiness, their ability to survive attack, and the flexibility and sureness with which we can control them to achieve our national purpose and strategic objectives.

6. The strength and deployment of our forces in combination with those of our allies should be sufficiently powerful and mobile to prevent the steady erosion of the free world through limited wars; and it is this role that should constitute the primary mission of our overseas forces. Nonnuclear wars, and sublimited or guerrilla warfare, have since 1945 constituted the most active and constant threat to free world security. Those units of our forces which are stationed overseas, or are designed to fight overseas, can be most usefully

oriented toward deterring or confining those conflicts which do not justify and must not lead to a general nuclear attack. In the event of a major aggression that could not be repulsed by conventional forces, we must be prepared to take whatever action with whatever weapons are appropriate. But our objective now is to increase our ability to confine our response to nonnuclear weapons, and to lessen the incentive for any limited aggression by making clear what our response will accomplish. In most areas of the world, the main burden of local defense against overt attack, subversion and guerrilla warfare must rest on local populations and forces. But given the great likelihood and seriousness of this threat, we must be prepared to make a substantial contribution in the form of strong, highly mobile forces trained in this type of warfare, some of which must be deployed in forward areas, with a substantial airlift and sealift capacity and prestocked overseas bases.

7. Our defense posture must be both flexible and determined. Any potential aggressor contemplating an attack on any part of the free world with any kind of weapons, conventional or nuclear, must know that our response will be suitable, selective, swift and effective. While he may be uncertain of its exact nature and location, there must be no uncertainty about our determination and capacity to take whatever steps are necessary to meet our obligations. We must be able to make deliberate choices in weapons and strategy, shift the tempo of our production and alter the direction of our forces to meet rapidly changing conditions or objectives at very short notice and under any circumstances. Our weapons systems must be usable in a manner permitting deliberation and discrimination as to timing, scope and targets

in response to civilian authority; and our defenses must be secure against prolonged reattack as well as a surprise first strike. To purchase productive capacity and to initiate development programs that may never need to be used, as this budget proposes, adopts an insurance policy of buying alternative future options.

8. Our defense posture must be designed to reduce the danger of irrational or unpremeditated general war, the danger of an unnecessary escalation of a small war into a large one, or of miscalculation or misinterpretation of an incident or enemy intention. Our diplomatic efforts to reach agreements on the prevention of surprise attack, an end to the spread of nuclear weapons, indeed all our efforts to end the arms race, are aimed at this objective. We shall strive for improved communication among all nations, to make clear our own intentions and resolution, and to prevent any nation from underestimating the response of any other, as has too often happened in the past. In addition, our own military activities must be safeguarded against the possibility of inadvertent triggering incidents. But even more importantly, we must make certain that our retaliatory power does not rest on decisions made in ambiguous circumstances, or permit a catastrophic mistake.

It would not be appropriate at this time or in this message either to boast of our strength or to dwell upon our needs and dangers. It is sufficient to say that the budgetary recommendations which follow, together with other policy, organizational and related changes and studies now under way administratively, are designed to provide for an increased strength, flexi-

bility and control in our defense establishment in accordance
with the above policies. . . .

*The remainder of the President's message sketched out his
detailed recommendations with respect to the defense budget.
The message concluded as follows:*

Our military position today is strong. But positive action must
be taken now if we are to have the kind of forces we will need
for our security in the future. Our preparation against danger
is our hope of safety. The changes in the defense program
which I have recommended will greatly enhance the security
of this nation in the perilous years which lie ahead. It is not
pleasant to request additional funds at this time for national
security. Our interest, as I have emphasized, lies in peaceful
solutions, in reducing tension, in settling disputes at the conference table and not on the battlefield. I am hopeful that
these policies will help secure these ends. I commend them to
the Congress and to the nation.

THE MEANS OF SELF-DEFENSE

Two months later, in his second State of the Union message, the President returned to the subject of defense.

A NETWORK OF ALLIANCES

Special Message to the Congress on Urgent National Needs, May 25, 1961

But while we talk of sharing and building and the competition of ideas, others talk of arms and threaten war. So we have learned to keep our defenses strong, and to co-operate with others in a partnership of self-defense. The events of recent weeks have caused us to look anew at these efforts.

The center of freedom's defense is our network of world alliances, extending from the North Atlantic Treaty Organization, recommended by a Democratic President and approved by a Republican Congress, to the Southeast Asia Treaty Organization, recommended by a Republican President and approved by a Democratic Congress. These alliances were constructed in the 1940's and 1950's; it is our task and responsibility in the sixties to strengthen them.

To meet the changing conditions of power, and power relationships have changed, we have endorsed an increased emphasis on NATO conventional strength. At the same time we are affirming our conviction that the NATO nuclear deterrent must also be kept strong. I have made clear our intention to commit to the NATO command, for this purpose, the five Polaris submarines originally suggested by President Eisenhower, with the possibility, if needed, of more to come.

Second, a major part of our partnership for self-defense is the Military Assistance Program. The main burden of local defense against local attack, subversion, insurrection or guerrilla warfare must of necessity rest with local forces. Where these forces have the necessary will and capacity to cope with such threats, our intervention is rarely necessary or helpful. Where the will is present and only capacity is lacking, our Military Assistance Program can be of help.

But this program, like economic assistance, needs a new emphasis. It cannot be extended without regard to the social, political and military reforms essential to internal respect and stability. The equipment and training provided must be tailored to legitimate local needs and to our own foreign and military policies, not to our supply of military stocks or a local leader's desire for military display. And military assistance can, in addition to its military purposes, make a contribution to economic progress, as do our own Army Engineers. . . .

I . . . request the Congress to provide a total of $1.885 billion for military assistance in the coming fiscal year, an amount less than that requested a year ago, but a minimum which must be assured if we are to help those nations make secure their independence. . . .

OUR OWN MILITARY AND INTELLIGENCE SHIELD

. . . I have directed a further reinforcement of our own capacity to deter or resist nonnuclear aggression. In the conventional field, with one exception, I find no present need for large new levies of men. What is needed is rather a change of position to give us still further increases in flexibility.

Therefore, I am directing the Secretary of Defense to undertake a reorganization and modernization of the Army's divisional structure, to increase its nonnuclear firepower, to improve its tactical mobility in any environment, to insure its flexibility to meet any direct or indirect threat, to facilitate its co-ordination with our major allies, and to provide more modern mechanized divisions in Europe and bring our equipment up to date, and new airborne brigades in both the Pacific and Europe.

And second, I am asking the Congress for an additional $100 million to begin the procurement task necessary to re-equip this new Army structure with the most modern material. . . .

Third, I am directing the Secretary of Defense to expand rapidly and substantially, in co-operation with our allies, the orientation of existing forces for the conduct of nonnuclear war, paramilitary operations and sublimited or unconventional wars.

In addition, our special forces and unconventional warfare units will be increased and reoriented. Throughout the services new emphasis must be placed on the special skills and languages which are required to work with local populations.

Fourth, the Army is developing plans to make possible a much more rapid deployment of a major portion of its highly trained reserve forces. . . .

Fifth, to enhance the already formidable ability of the Marine Corps to respond to limited war emergencies, I am asking the Congress for $60 million to increase Marine Corps strength to 190,000 men. . . .

Finally, to cite one other area of activities that are both legitimate and necessary as a means of self-defense in an age of hidden perils, our whole intelligence effort must be reviewed, and its co-ordination with other elements of policy assured. . . .

CIVIL DEFENSE

One major element of the national security program which this nation has never squarely faced up to is Civil Defense. This problem arises not from present trends but from national inaction in which most of us have participated. In the past decade we have intermittently considered a variety of programs, but we have never adopted a consistent policy. Public consideration has been largely characterized by apathy, indifference and skepticism while, at the same time, many of the Civil Defense plans have been so far-reaching and unrealistic that they have not gained essential support.

This Administration has been looking hard at exactly what Civil Defense can and cannot do. It cannot be obtained cheaply. It cannot give an assurance of blast protection that will be proof against surprise attack or guaranteed against obsolescence or destruction. And it cannot deter a nuclear attack.

We will deter an enemy from making a nuclear attack only if our retaliatory power is so strong and so invulnerable that he knows he would be destroyed by our response. If we have that strength, Civil Defense is not needed to deter an attack. If we should ever lack it, Civil Defense would not be an adequate substitute.

But this deterrent concept assumes rational calculations by

rational men. And the history of this planet, and particularly the history of the twentieth century, is sufficient to remind us of the possibilities of an irrational attack, a miscalculation, an accidental war, or a war of escalation in which the stakes by each side gradually increase to the point of maximum danger which cannot be either foreseen or deterred. It is on this basis that Civil Defense can be readily justifiable, as insurance for the civilian population in case of an enemy miscalculation. It is insurance we trust will never be needed, but insurance which we could never forgive ourselves for foregoing in the event of catastrophe.

Once the validity of this concept is recognized, there is no point in delaying the initiation of a nation-wide, long-range program of identifying present fallout shelter capacity and providing shelter in new and existing structures. Such a program would protect millions of people against the hazards of radioactive fallout in the event of a large-scale nuclear attack. Effective performance of the entire program requires not only new legislative authority and more funds, but also sound organizational arrangements.

Therefore, under the authority vested in me by Reorganization Plan No. 1 of 1958, I am assigning responsibility for this program to the top civilian authority already responsible for continental defense, the Secretary of Defense. It is important that this function remain civilian, in nature and leadership, and this feature will not be changed. . . .

In a speech on July 25 the President again spoke of the needs of civil defense:

Report to the Nation on Berlin,
July 25, 1961

. . . To recognize the possibilities of nuclear war in the missile age, without our citizens knowing what they should do and where they should go if bombs begin to fall, would be a failure of responsibility. In May, I pledged a new start on Civil Defense. Last week, I assigned, on the recommendation of the Civil Defense Director, basic responsibility for this program to the Secretary of Defense, to make certain it is administered and co-ordinated with our continental defense efforts at the highest civilian level. Tomorrow, I am requesting of the Congress new funds for the following immediate objectives: to identify and mark space in existing structures, public and private, that could be used for fallout shelters in case of attack; to stock those shelters with food, water, first-aid kits and other minimum essentials for survival; to increase their capacity; to improve our air-raid warning and fallout detection systems, including a new household warning system which is now under development; and to take other measures that will be effective at an early date to save millions of lives if needed.

In the event of an attack, the lives of those families which are not hit in a nuclear blast and fire can still be saved—*if* they can be warned to take shelter and *if* that shelter is available. We owe that kind of insurance to our families, and to our country. In contrast to our friends in Europe, the need for this kind of protection is new to our shores. But the time to start is now. In the coming months, I hope to let every citizen know what steps he can take without delay to protect his family in case of attack. I know that you will want to do no less.

The addition of $207 million in Civil Defense appropriations brings our total new defense budget requests to $3.454 billion, and a total of $47.5 billion for the year. This is an increase in the defense budget of $6 billion since January, and has resulted in official estimates of a budget deficit of over $5 billion. The Secretary of the Treasury and other economic advisers assure me, however, that our economy has the capacity to bear this new request.

CHAPTER V
SPACE

"NOW IT IS . . . TIME FOR A GREAT NEW AMERICAN ENTERPRISE, TIME FOR THIS NATION TO TAKE A CLEARLY LEADING ROLE IN SPACE ACHIEVEMENT, WHICH IN MANY WAYS MAY HOLD THE KEY TO OUR FUTURE ON EARTH."

". . . THIS IS NOT MERELY A RACE. SPACE IS OPEN TO US NOW; AND OUR EAGERNESS TO SHARE ITS MEANING IS NOT GOVERNED BY THE EFFORTS OF OTHERS. WE GO INTO SPACE BECAUSE WHATEVER MANKIND MUST UNDERTAKE, FREE MEN MUST FULLY SHARE."

"LET IT BE CLEAR THAT I AM ASKING THE CONGRESS AND THE COUNTRY TO ACCEPT A FIRM COMMITMENT TO A NEW COURSE OF ACTION, A COURSE WHICH WILL LAST FOR MANY YEARS AND CARRY VERY HEAVY COSTS. . . . IF WE ARE TO GO ONLY HALFWAY, OR REDUCE OUR SIGHTS IN THE FACE OF DIFFICULTY . . . IT WOULD BE BETTER NOT TO GO AT ALL."

Throughout 1961, the Soviet Union continued to hold a commanding lead in important aspects of space technology. On April 12, the Russians sent the first man into orbit. On August 6 they did it again. In the meantime, the United States had to be content with sending two men on suborbital space flights. Two press-conference comments by the President reveal something of the Administration's thinking on this question. In February, the President told reporters:

We are very concerned that we do not put a man in space in order to gain some additional prestige, and have the man take a disproportionate risk, so we are going to be extremely careful in our work; and even if we should come in second in putting a man in space, I will still be satisfied if, when we finally put a man in space, his chances of survival are as high as I think they must be.

On April 12—the date of the first Soviet launching—a reporter again raised the subject and received a straightforward reply:

QUESTION: Mr. President, a Member of Congress said today that he was tired of seeing the United States second to Russia in the space field. . . . What is the prospect that we will catch up with Russia and perhaps surpass Russia in this field?

THE PRESIDENT: Well, the Soviet Union gained an important advantage by securing . . . large boosters, which were able to put up greater weights, and that advantage is going to be with them for some time. However tired of it anybody may be, and no one is more tired of it than I am, it is a fact that it is going to take some time, and I think we have to recognize it. . . . We are, I hope, going to be able to carry out our efforts, with due regard to the problem of the life of the man involved, this year. But we are behind.

I am sure they are making a concentrated effort to stay ahead. We have provided additional emphasis on Saturn. We have provided additional emphasis on Rover. We are attempting to improve other systems which will give us a stronger position, all of which are very expensive, all of which involve billions of dollars.

So in answer to your question, as I said in my State of the Union Message, the news will be worse before it is better, and it will be some time before we catch up. We are, I hope, going to go in other areas where we can be first, and which will bring perhaps more long-range benefits to mankind. But here we are behind.

Then in May President Kennedy had the pleasant duty of honoring the first American astronaut.

Remarks to Commander Alan B. Shepard,
May 8, 1961

I want to express on behalf of all of us the great pleasure we have in welcoming Commander Shepard and Mrs. Shepard here today. I think they know as citizens of this great country how proud we are of him, what satisfaction we take in his accomplishment, what a service he has rendered our country. And we are also very proud of Mrs. Shepard.

I know that the other members of this team who are astronauts know that our pride in them is equal. Commander Shepard has pointed out . . . that this was a common effort in which a good many men were involved. I think it does credit to him that he is associated with such a distinguished group of Americans whom we are all glad to honor today—his companions in the flight into outer space—so I think we want to give them all a hand. They are the tanned and healthy ones; the others are Washington employees. . . .

And I also want to take cognizance of the fact that this flight was made out in the open with all the possibilities of failure, which would have been damaging to our country's prestige. Because great risks were taken in that regard, it seems to me that we have some right to claim that this open society of ours which risked much, gained much.

Late in May the President made his most important statement of the year on Administration policy with respect to space.

Special Message to the Congress on Urgent National Needs,
May 25, 1961

If we are to win the battle that is now going on around the world between freedom and tyranny, the dramatic achievements in space which occurred in recent weeks should have made clear to us all, as did the Sputnik in 1957, the impact of this adventure on the minds of men everywhere, who are attempting to make a determination of which road they should take. Since early in my term, our efforts in space have been under review. With the advice of the Vice President, who is Chairman of the National Space Council, we have examined where we are strong and where we are not, where we may succeed and where we may not. Now it is time to take longer strides, time for a great new American enterprise, time for this nation to take a clearly leading role in space achievement, which in many ways may hold the key to our future on earth.

I believe we possess all the resources and talents necessary. But the facts of the matter are that we have never made the national decisions or marshaled the national resources required for such leadership. We have never specified long-range goals on an urgent time schedule, or managed our resources and our time so as to insure their fulfillment.

Recognizing the head start obtained by the Soviets with their large rocket engines, which gives them many months of lead-time, and recognizing the likelihood that they will exploit this lead for some time to come in still more impressive successes, we nevertheless are required to make new efforts on our own. For while we cannot guarantee that we shall one day be first, we can guarantee that any failure to make this effort will make us last. We take an additional risk by making it in full view of the world, but as shown by the feat of Astronaut Shepard, this very risk enhances our stature when we are successful. But this is not merely a race. Space is open to us now; and our eagerness to share its meaning is not governed by the efforts of others. We go into space because whatever mankind must undertake, free men must fully share.

I therefore ask the Congress, above and beyond the increases I have earlier requested for space activities, to provide the funds which are needed to meet the following national goals:

First, I believe that this nation should commit itself to

achieving the goal, before this decade is out, of landing a man on the moon and returning him safely to the earth. No single space project in this period will be more impressive to mankind, or more important for the long-range exploration of space; and none will be so difficult or expensive to accomplish. We propose to accelerate development of the appropriate lunar space craft. We propose to develop alternate liquid and solid fuel boosters, much larger than any now being developed, until we are certain which is superior. We propose additional funds for other engine developments and for unmanned explorations, explorations which are particularly important for one purpose which this nation will never overlook: the survival of the man who first makes this daring flight. But in a very real sense, it will not be one man going to the moon; if we make this judgment affirmatively, it will be an entire nation. For all of us must work to put him there.

Second, an additional $23 million, together with $7 million already available, to accelerate development of the Rover nuclear rocket. This gives promise of someday providing a means for even more exciting and ambitious exploration of space, perhaps beyond the moon, perhaps to the very end of the solar system itself.

Third, an additional $50 million will make the most of our present leadership, by accelerating the use of space satellites for world-wide communications.

Fourth, an additional $75 million, of which $53 million is for the Weather Bureau, will help give us at the earliest possible time a satellite system for world-wide weather observation.

Let it be clear—and this is a judgment which the Members of Congress must finally make—let it be clear that I am asking the Congress and the country to accept a firm commitment to a new course of action, a course which will last for many years and carry very heavy costs of $531 million in fiscal 1962, an estimated $7 billion to $9 billion additional over the next five years. If we are to go only halfway, or reduce our sights in the face of difficulty, in my judgment it would be better not to go at all.

Now this is a choice which this country must make, and I am confident that under the leadership of the Space Committees of the Congress, and the Appropriating Committees, you will consider the matter carefully.

It is a most important decision that we make as a nation. But all of you have lived through the last four years and have seen the significance of space and the adventures in space, and no one can predict with certainty what the ultimate meaning will be of mastery of space.

I believe we should go to the moon. But I think every citizen of this country as well as the Members of the Congress should consider the matter carefully in making their judgment, to which we have given attention over many weeks and months, because it is a heavy burden, and there is no sense in agreeing or desiring that the United States take an affirmative position in outer space, unless we are prepared to do the work and bear the burdens to make it successful. If we are not, we should decide today. . . .

This decision demands a major national commitment of scientific and technical manpower, material and facilities, and the possibility of their diversion from other important activities where they are already thinly spread. It means a degree of dedication, organization and discipline which have not always characterized our research and development efforts. It means we cannot afford undue work stoppages, inflated costs of material or talent, wasteful interagency rivalries, or a high turnover of key personnel.

New objectives and new money cannot solve these problems. They could, in fact, aggravate them further, unless every scientist, every engineer, every serviceman, every technician, contractor and civil servant gives his personal pledge that this nation will move forward, with the full speed of freedom, in the exciting adventure of space.

CHAPTER VI
THE ECONOMY

"ANYONE WHO IS HONESTLY SEEKING A JOB AND CAN'T FIND IT DESERVES THE ATTENTION OF THE UNITED STATES GOVERNMENT AND THE PEOPLE. . . ."

". . . OUR PROGRAMS MUST AIM AT EXPANDING AMERICAN PRODUCTIVE CAPACITY AT A RATE THAT SHOWS THE WORLD THE VIGOR AND VITALITY OF A FREE ECONOMY."

". . . OUR REVENUES AND THUS OUR SUCCESS ARE DEPENDENT UPON YOUR [BUSINESS] PROFITS AND YOUR SUCCESS. . . . FAR FROM BEING NATURAL ENEMIES, GOVERNMENT AND BUSINESS ARE NECESSARY ALLIES."

"AS RECOVERY PROGRESSES, THERE WILL BE TEMPTATIONS TO SEEK UNJUSTIFIED PRICE AND WAGE INCREASES. THESE WE CANNOT AFFORD."

The economic recession of 1960 continued on into the winter and was still very much in evidence at the time of President Kennedy's inauguration. It had been the topic of some lively campaign discussions, and the President had expressed his views with vigor. Two weeks after the Inauguration he sent to the Congress his Message on Economic Recovery and Growth.

ECONOMIC RECOVERY

Message to the Congress on Economic Recovery and Growth, February 2, 1961

America has the human and material resources to meet the demands of national security and the obligations of world leadership while at the same time advancing well-being at home. But our nation has been falling further and further short of its economic capabilities.

In the past seven years, our rate of growth has slowed down disturbingly. In the past three and one-half years, the gap between what we can produce and what we do produce has threatened to become chronic.

And in the past year, our economic problem has been aggravated by recession and by loss of gold. I shall shortly send to the Congress a separate message dealing with our international balance of payments and gold position.

The nation cannot, and will not, be satisfied with economic decline and slack. The United States cannot afford, in this time of national need and world crisis, to dissipate its opportunities for economic growth. We cannot expect to make good in a day or even a year the accumulated deficiencies of several years.

But realistic aims for 1961 are to reverse the downtrend in our economy, to narrow the gap of unused potential, to abate the waste and misery of unemployment and at the same time to maintain reasonable stability of the price level.

For 1962 and 1963 our programs must aim at expanding American productive capacity at a rate that shows the world the vigor and vitality of a free economy. These are not merely fond hopes; they are realistic goals. We pledge and ask maximum effort for their attainment. . . .

The potential of the American economy is constantly expanding. The labor force is rising by 1.5 per cent per year. Output per man rises annually by 2 per cent as a result of new and better plant and equipment, modern technology and improved human skills. These increases in manpower and productivity provide the base for a potential annual growth of 3.5 per cent in the nation's total output. This is not high enough. Our potential growth rate can and should be increased. To do so, we propose to expand the nation's investments in physical and human resources, and in science and technology. . . .

An unbalanced economy does not produce a balanced budget. The Treasury's pocketbook suffers when the economy performs poorly. Lower incomes earned by households and corporations are reflected in lower Federal tax receipts. Assistance to unemployed workers and the costs of other measures for alleviation of economic distress are certain to rise as business declines. That is why recession, as our $12 billion deficit in the fiscal year 1959 recently reminded us, forces the budget into imbalance. That is why the prospect of surpluses in the Federal budgets for fiscal 1961 and fiscal 1962 is fading away.

The Federal budget can and should be made an instrument of prosperity and stability, not a deterrent to recovery. This Administration is pledged to a Federal revenue system that balances the budget over the years of the economic cycle, yielding surpluses for debt retirement in times of high employment that more than offset the deficits which accompany, and indeed help overcome, low levels of economic activity in poor years. . . .

The programs I am now proposing will not by themselves unbalance the budget which was earlier submitted, but are designed to fulfill our responsibility to alleviate distress and speed recovery, both through benefits directly available to needy persons and through desirable fiscal effects on the economy. They will sustain consumer spending and increase aggregate demand now when the economy is slack. Many of these expenditures will automatically cease when high employment and production are restored.

Other measures contained in this message propose necessary uses of national economic capacity and tax revenue for our long-range growth, and are essential even in the absence of a recession. They are proposed because the country needs them, can afford them and would indeed be poorer without them. . . .

Rapid technological change is resulting in serious employment dislocations, which deny us the full stimulus to growth which advancing technology makes possible. Labor and industry have demonstrated co-operative initiative in working out solutions in specific plants and industries. Government action is also necessary, not only to maintain an environment favorable to economic growth, but also to deal with special problems in communities and industries suffering from economic dislocations and to help those who through unemployment are bearing an unfair share of the burden of technological change. . . .

Government can help further by encouraging labor and management to find ways to smooth the adjustment to technological change and thus to maintain and reinforce the favorable attitude toward economic progress that characterizes American business and labor alike.

Accordingly, I shall issue an Executive Order establishing the President's Advisory Committee on Labor-Management Policy, with members drawn from labor, management and the public. The committee is directed to advise the President with respect to actions that may be taken by labor, management and the public which will promote free and responsible collective bargaining, industrial peace, sound wage policies, sound price policies and stability, a higher standard of living, increased productivity and America's competitive position in world markets.

It will consider national manpower needs and the special benefits and problems created by automation and other technological advances. I look to the committee to make an important contribution to labor-management relations and an understanding of their importance to the stability of prices and the health of the economy.

The course of the American price level depends in substantial measure on wage and price decisions of labor and management. This dependence grows in importance as the economy moves toward full employment. All of us must now be conscious of the need for policies that enable American goods to compete successfully with foreign goods.

We cannot afford unsound wage and price movements which push up costs, weaken our international competitive position, restrict job opportunities and jeopardize the health of our domestic economy.

Price stability will also be aided by the adoption of a tax incentive plan mentioned earlier, which will encourage a higher rate of business investment in improved plants and equipment.

Price increases for many products and services have occurred because these industries have lagged behind in the march of productivity and technological advance. Indeed, in the present economic situation, a stepping-up of productivity improvement throughout the economy would contribute to the achievement of price stability.

We must not as a nation come to accept the proposition that reasonable price stability can be achieved only by tolerating a slack economy, chronic unemployment and a creeping rate of growth.

Neither will we seek to buy short-run economic gains by paying the price of excessive increases in the cost of living. Always a cruel tax upon the weak, inflation is now the certain road to a balance of payments crisis and the disruption of the international economy of the Western world.

Inflation has no single cause. There have been times in the postwar period when prices rose sharply in response to a rate of total spending in excess of our capacity to produce. The government will not contribute to this process, and we shall use the powerful tools of fiscal and monetary policy to arrest any such movement if it should threaten in the year ahead.

Some price increases, particularly among the consumer services, have been caused by the failure of productive resources to move promptly in response to basic shifts in the pattern of demand. We shall seek means to encourage the movement of manpower and capital into sectors of expanding demand. . . .

Elsewhere in the message the President announced that he would propose modifications of business taxes to stimulate investment in plant and equipment. In addition, the President:

1. Recommended changes in the Social Security program to (a) raise the minimum monthly retirement benefit, (b) begin payments to men at age 62, (c) liberalize the eligibility requirements, (d) increase benefits to aged widows, and (e) broaden disability-insurance protection.

2. Recommended increasing the minimum wage and extending coverage to several million workers not then covered.

3. Recommended temporary extension of unemployment insurance benefits and permanent reforms of the Federal-State unemployment insurance system.

4. Announced that the Administration's objectives in monetary policy and debt management would be (a) to check declines in short-term interest rates that would lead to a further outflow of funds abroad, and at the same time (b) to promote the decline of long-term interest rates.

5. Announced (a) a reduction in the maximum permissible interest rates on loans insured by the Federal Housing Administration and lower interest on loans made by the Community Facilities Administration and (b) a speed-up in the initiation and completion of projects under the Housing and Home Finance Agency; and urged a general reduction of mortgage rates.

6. Recommended area-redevelopment legislation to aid areas of heavy chronic unemployment.

7. Announced the expansion of surplus-food distribution and initiation of pilot food-stamp programs in six states.

8. Announced earlier payment of the Veterans Administration 1961 insurance dividends.

9. *Announced directives to Federal agencies to accelerate procurement and construction programs, and to give preference in these programs to areas of labor surplus.*

10. *Announced a directive to expand counseling and placement functions of the U.S. Employment Service.*

11. *Asked Congress to enact an interim amendment to the Aid to Dependent Children program to include the children of the needy unemployed.*

Of the economic recovery measures which the President considered urgent, Congress passed legislation dealing with temporary extension of unemployment benefits, aid to dependent children, aid to depressed areas, changes in the Social Security program, and an increase in the minimum wage.

BUSINESS AND GOVERNMENT

Some elements within the business community made no secret of their conviction that the new Administration was unfriendly to business. In a speech to the National Industrial Conference Board three weeks after his Inauguration, President Kennedy sought to correct this impression.

Address to the National Industrial Conference Board,
February 13, 1961

. . . I want, first of all, to express my personal thanks to all of you for having come to our city, and for participating in what I hope will be a most useful and helpful proceeding which will benefit this government and our country.

It has recently been suggested that whether I serve one or two terms in the Presidency, I will find myself at the end of that period at what might be called the awkward age, too old to begin a new career and too young to write my memoirs.

A similar dilemma, it seems to me, is posed by the occasion of a Presidential address to a business group on business conditions less than four weeks after entering the White House, for it is too early to be claiming credit for the new Administration and too late to be blaming the old one. And it would be premature to seek your support in the next election, and inaccurate to express thanks for having had it in the last one.

I feel, nevertheless, that I can claim kinship here, and have that claim allowed. For I am convinced that the real spirit of American business is not represented by those involved in price-fixing, conflict-of-interest or collusion. The real spirit is in this room, in your recognition of your public responsibilities, your pursuit of the truth, your desire for better industrial relations, better technological progress and better price stability and economic growth. And because your organization portrays *that* picture of American business, I am delighted and proud to be here with you.

The complaint has often been made in business circles that the Federal Government is a silent partner in every corporation, taking roughly half of all of your net earnings without risk to itself. But it should be also realized that this makes business a not always silent partner of the Federal Government, that our revenues and thus our success are dependent upon your profits and your success, and that, far from being natural enemies, government and business are necessary allies.

For example, the 1960 drop in expected corporate profits of some $6 billion to $7 billion also caused a loss in Federal revenues of over $3 billion—enough to pay the Federal share of all of our antirecession, health and education proposals for the next fiscal year and still have enough left over to start closing what the Democrats in this Administration used to call "The Missile Gap."

An equally critical gap separates the tax revenues of a lagging economy from those which are potentially within our grasp: a gap of at least $12 billion. Even after we are able to launch every program necessary for national security and development, this amount of revenue would still leave a substantial surplus, a surplus essential to help defend our economy against inflation, and, equally important, a surplus that, when applied to the Federal debt, would free additional savings for business investment and expansion.

In short, there is no inevitable clash between the public and private sectors, or between investment and consumption, nor, as I have said, between government and business. All elements in our national economic growth are interdependent. Each must play its proper role, and that is the hope and the aim of this Administration.

If those of you who are in the world of business and we who are in the world of government are necessarily partners, what kind of partnership is this going to be? Will it be marked by mutual suspicion and recrimination or by mutual understanding and fruitful collaboration?

On behalf of my associates in the Cabinet, I want to be very precise: We will not discriminate for or against any segment of our society, or any segment of the business community. We are vigorously opposed to corruption and monopoly and human exploitation, but we are not opposed to business.

We know that your success and ours are intertwined, that you have facts and know-how that we need. Whatever past differences may have existed, we seek more than an attitude of truce, more than a treaty; we seek the spirit of a full-fledged alliance. . . .

HOUSING AND COMMUNITY DEVELOPMENT

On March 9, the President sent to Congress another major piece of his domestic program—his plans for housing and community development.

Special Message on Housing and Community Development, March 9, 1961

Our communities are what we make them. We as a nation have before us the opportunity, and the responsibility, to remold our cities, to improve our patterns of community development, and to provide for the housing needs of all segments of our population. . . .

In 1949 the Congress, with great vision, announced our national housing policy of "a decent home and a suitable living environment for every American family." We have progressed since that time; but we must still redeem this pledge to the 14 million American families who currently live in substandard or deteriorating homes, and protect the other 39 million American families from the encroachment of blight and slums.

An equal challenge is the tremendous urban growth that lies ahead. Within fifteen years our population will rise to 235 million and by the year 2000 to 300 million people. Most of this increase will occur in and around urban areas. We must begin now to lay the foundation for livable, efficient and attractive communities of the future.

Land adjoining urban centers has been engulfed by urban development at the astounding rate of about one million acres a year. But the result has been haphazard and inefficient suburban expansion, and continued setbacks in the central cities' desperate struggle against blight and decay. Their social and economic base has been eroded by the movement of middle- and upper-income families to the suburbs, by the attendant loss of retail sales, and by the preference of many industrial firms for outlying locations.

Our policy for housing and community development must be directed toward the accomplishment of three basic national objectives:

First, to renew our cities and assure sound growth of our rapidly expanding metropolitan areas.

Second, to provide decent housing for all of our people.

Third, to encourage a prosperous and efficient construction industry as an essential component of general economic prosperity and growth.

The housing industry is one of the largest employers of labor. Residential construction alone accounts for 30 per cent of total private investment in this country. The housing market absorbs more private credit than any other single sector of the economy. Other important industries and services, including those concerned with building materials, appliances, furniture and home improvement, depend largely and directly on new housing construction. . . .

. . . The housing market today is basically different from that of only a few years ago. There is no longer an enormous backlog of economic demand which can be released simply by providing ample credit. Credit devices must now be used selectively to encourage private industry to build and finance more housing in the lower price ranges to meet the unfilled demands of moderate-income families. It is these families who offer the largest and the most immediate potential housing market, along with those of still lower incomes who must rely on low-rent public housing.

There are eight million families today with incomes of less than $2,500, seven million more with incomes between $2,500 and $4,000. Among the nineteen million individuals who live alone, nearly 50 per cent have incomes of less than $1,500. One-third of the six million nonwhite households live in substandard housing. And our older citizens, a group growing at the rate of 500,000 each year, have special housing needs. And in addition to all of this, before this decade is out, a rate of construction of at least two million new homes a year will be required merely to meet the needs of new family units being formed. . . .

Seventy-three out of 258 central cities lost population in the decade of the fifties, when our urban population as a whole grew rapidly. Other powerful trends have been eroding the central cities over a much longer period.

. . . If the cities are to recapture their economic health, they must offer better opportunities for those commercial, industrial and residential developments for which their central position is a distinct advantage. They must strengthen their cultural and recreational facilities and thus attract more middle- and upper-income residents. They should make space available for suitable light industries, especially those which need close-in locations. And they must improve their transportation systems, particularly rapid transit services.

Urban renewal programs to date have been too narrow to cope effectively with the basic problems facing older cities. We must do more than concern ourselves with bad housing; we must reshape our cities into effective nerve centers for expanding metropolitan areas. Our urban renewal efforts must be substantially reoriented from slum clearance and slum prevention into positive programs for economic and social regeneration. . . .

Land is the most precious resource of the metropolitan area. The present patterns of haphazard suburban development are contributing to a tragic waste in the use of a vital resource now being consumed at an alarming rate.

Open space must be reserved to provide parks and recreation, conserve water and other natural resources, prevent building in undesirable locations, prevent erosion and floods, and avoid the wasteful extension of public services. Open land is also needed to provide reserves for future residential development, to protect against undue speculation, and to make it possible for state and regional bodies to control the rate and character of community development. . . .

In other parts of the message, the President recommended:
1. The establishment of a Cabinet-rank Department of Housing and Urban Affairs.

2. Authorizations totaling $2.5 billion over four years for urban renewal programs; liberalized relocation payments to businessmen displaced by such programs; and encouragement to communities to undertake long-term planning of their renewal needs.

3. A broadened program of FHA-insured, no-down-payment, forty-year home mortgages for middle-income families; and a new program of long-term, low-interest-rate loans for rental and co-operative housing.

4. Authorization for construction of 100,000 additional units of low-rent public housing for low-income families, half of these units to be earmarked for elderly people.

5. More liberal authority for FHA to insure home improvement loans; and partial subsidies for rehabilitation of slum areas.

6. Grants and loans for reservation or acquisition by communities of permanent "open space" for parks and other facilities; and loans to communities for construction of public facilities.

7. Extension and expansion of provisions for veterans' housing loans and loan guarantees; expansion of present direct loan authorization for housing of the elderly; and extension of farm housing loan authority.

8. Extension and expansion of Federal aid to urban and metropolitan planning; and intensified research and experimentation on housing and urban problems, the technology of home-building and urban transportation problems.

In June Congress passed an omnibus housing bill which fulfilled a great part of the President's requests. But a bill to establish the proposed Urban Affairs Department awaited action in 1962.

UNFINISHED TASKS

Toward the end of May, with economic recovery well on the way, the President spoke of the tasks yet to be done.

Special Message to the Congress on Urgent National Needs, May 25, 1961

The first and basic task confronting this nation this year was to turn recession into recovery. An affirmative antirecession program, initiated with your co-operation, supported the natural forces in the private sector; and our economy is now enjoying renewed confidence and energy. The recession has been halted. Recovery is under way.

But the task of abating unemployment and achieving a full use of our resources does remain a serious challenge for us all. Large-scale unemployment during a recession is bad enough; large-scale unemployment during a period of prosperity would be intolerable.

I am therefore transmitting to the Congress a new Manpower Development and Training program, to train or retrain several hundred thousand workers, particularly in those areas where we have seen chronic unemployment as a result of technological factors and new occupational skills, over a four-year period, in order to replace those skills made obsolete by automation and industrial change with the new skills which the new processes demand.

It should be a satisfaction to us all that we have made great strides in restoring world confidence in the dollar, halting the outflow of gold and improving our balance of payments. During the last two months, our gold stocks actually increased by $17 million, compared to a loss of $635 million during the last two months of 1960. We must maintain this progress, and this will require the co-operation and restraint of everyone. As recovery progresses, there will be temptations to seek unjustified price and wage increases. These we cannot afford. They will only handicap our efforts to compete abroad and to achieve full recovery here at home. Labor and management must, and I am confident that they will, pursue responsible wage and price policies in these critical times. I look to the President's Advisory Committee on Labor-Management Policy to give a strong lead in this direction.

Moreover, if the budget deficit now increased by the needs of our security is to be held within manageable proportions, it will be necessary to hold tightly to prudent fiscal standards; and I request the co-operation of the Congress in this regard: to refrain from adding funds or programs, desirable as they may be, to the budget; to end the postal deficit, as my predecessor also recommended, through increased rates—a deficit incidentally, this year, which exceeds the fiscal year 1962 cost of all the space and defense measures that I am submitting today; to provide full pay-as-you-go highway financing; and to close those tax loopholes earlier specified. Our security and progress cannot be cheaply purchased; and their price must be found in what we all forego as well as what we all must pay. . . .

CHAPTER VII
THE CONDUCT OF GOVERNMENT

"WE CAN AFFORD TO DO WHAT MUST BE DONE, PUBLICLY AND PRIVATELY, UP TO THE LIMIT OF OUR ECONOMIC CAPACITY, A LIMIT WE HAVE NOT EVEN APPROACHED FOR SEVERAL YEARS."

". . . EXPENSE-ACCOUNT LIVING HAS BECOME A BYWORD. . . . THE SLOGAN 'IT'S DEDUCTIBLE' SHOULD PASS FROM OUR SCENE."

". . . THE BASIS OF EFFECTIVE GOVERNMENT IS PUBLIC CONFIDENCE, AND THAT CONFIDENCE IS ENDANGERED WHEN ETHICAL STANDARDS FALTER OR APPEAR TO FALTER."

". . . PUBLIC OFFICIALS ARE NOT A GROUP APART. THEY INEVITABLY REFLECT THE MORAL TONE OF THE SOCIETY IN WHICH THEY LIVE."

In March the President sent to the Congress his Message on Budget and Fiscal Policy. An incoming President has relatively little leeway in his first budget message. He inherits his predecessor's budget, and there is not time for the thorough study which would have to precede major revisions of that budget. Nevertheless, the opening paragraphs of the budget message which appear below throw some light on the policies of the new Administration.

BASIC FISCAL POLICIES

Message to the Congress on Budget and Fiscal Policy,
March 24, 1961

This Administration intends to adhere during the course of its term of office to the following basic principles:

1. Federal revenue and expenditure levels must be adequate to meet effectively and efficiently those essential needs of the nation which require public support as well as, or in place of, private effort. We can afford to do what must be done, publicly and privately, up to the limit of our economic capacity, a limit we have not even approached for several years.

2. Federal revenues and expenditures—the Federal budget —should, apart from any threat to national security, be in balance over the years of the business cycle, running a deficit in years of recession, when revenues decline and the economy needs the stimulus of additional expenditures, and running a surplus in years of prosperity, thus curbing inflation, reducing the public debt and freeing funds for private investment.

3. Federal expenditure and revenue programs should contribute to economic growth and maximum employment within a setting of reasonable price stability. Because of the limits which our balance of payments deficit currently places upon the use of monetary policy, especially the lowering of short-term interest rates, as a means of stimulating economic growth and employment, fiscal policy—our budget and tax policies— must assume a heavier share of the responsibility.

4. Each expenditure proposed will be evaluated in terms of our national needs and priorities, consistent with the limita-

tions and objectives described above and compared with the urgency of other budgetary requirements. We will not waste our resources on inefficient or undesirable expenditures simply because the economy is slack; nor, in order to run a surplus, will we deny our people essential services or security simply because the economy is prosperous.

5. As the nation, its needs and their complexity continue to grow, Federal nondefense expenditures may also be expected to increase, as predicted by a 1960 Bureau of the Budget study, and as indicated by the nearly 45 per cent increase from fiscal 1953 to fiscal 1961 in expenditures other than national security. But we must not allow expenditures to rise of their own momentum, without regard to value received, prospective revenues, economic conditions, the possibilities of closing out old activities when initiating new ones, and the weight of current taxes on the individual citizen and the economy. It is my determined purpose to be a prudent steward of the public funds, to obtain a dollar's worth of results for every dollar we spend. . . .

TAXATION

*Of more direct interest to the average American was the
message entitled "Our Federal Tax System" which the
President sent to the Congress on April 20.*

*Message to the Congress on the Federal Tax System,
April 20, 1961*

A strong and sound Federal tax system is essential to America's future. Without such a system, we cannot maintain our defenses and give leadership to the free world. Without such a system, we cannot render the public services necessary for enriching the lives of our people and furthering the growth of our economy.

The tax system must be adequate to meet our public needs. It must meet them fairly, calling on each of us to contribute his proper share to the cost of government. It must encourage efficient use of our resources. It must promote economic stability and stimulate economic growth. Economic expansion in turn creates a growing tax base, thus increasing revenue and thereby enabling us to meet more readily our public needs, as well as our needs as private individuals.

This message recognizes the basic soundness of our tax structure. But it also recognizes the changing needs and standards of our economic and international position, and the constructive reform needs to keep our tax system up to date and to maintain its equity. . . .

The elimination of certain defects and inequities as proposed below will provide revenue gains to offset the tax reductions offered to stimulate the economy. Thus no net loss of revenue is involved in this set of proposals. I wish to emphasize here that they are a "set"—and that considerations of both revenue and equity, as well as the interrelationship of many of the proposals, urge their consideration as a unit. . . .

LONG-RANGE TAX REFORM

While it is essential that the Congress receive at this time this Administration's proposals for urgent and obvious tax adjustments needed to fulfill the aims listed above, time has not permitted the comprehensive review necessary for a tax structure which is so complicated and so critically important to so many people. This message is but a first though urgent step along the road to constructive reform.

I am directing the Secretary of the Treasury, building on recent tax studies of the Congress, to undertake the research and preparation of a comprehensive tax reform program to be placed before the next session of the Congress.

Progressing from these studies, particularly those of the Committee on Ways and Means and the Joint Economic Committee, the program should be aimed at providing a broader and more uniform tax base, together with an appropriate rate structure. We can thereby work toward the goal of a higher rate of economic growth, a more equitable tax structure and a simpler tax law. I know these objectives are shared by, and at this particular time of year acutely desired by, the vast majority of the American people.

In meeting the demands of war finance, the individual income tax moved from a selective tax imposed on the wealthy to the means by which the great majority of our citizens participate in paying for well over one-half of our total budget receipts. It is supplemented by the corporation income tax, which provides for another quarter of the total.

This emphasis on income taxation has been a sound development. But so many taxpayers have become so preoccupied with so many tax-saving devices that business decisions are interfered with, and the efficient functioning of the price system is distorted.

Moreover, special provisions have developed into an increasing source of preferential treatment to various groups. Whenever one taxpayer is permitted to pay less, someone else must be asked to pay more. The uniform distribution of the tax burden is thereby disturbed and higher rates are made necessary by the narrowing of the tax base. Of course, some departures from uniformity are needed to promote desirable social or economic objectives of overriding importance which can be achieved most effectively through the tax mechanism. But many of the preferences which have developed do not meet such a test and need to be re-evaluated in our tax reform program.

It will be a major aim of our tax reform program to reverse this process by broadening the tax base and reconsidering the rate structure. The result should be a tax system that is more equitable, more efficient and more conducive to economic growth.

TAX INCENTIVE FOR MODERNIZATION AND EXPANSION

The history of our economy has been one of rising productivity, based on improvement in skills, advances in technology and a growing supply of more efficient tools and equipment. This rise has been reflected in rising wages and standards of living for our workers, as well as a healthy rate of growth for the economy as a whole. It has also been the foundation of our leadership in world markets, even as we enjoyed the highest wage rates in the world.

Today, as we face serious pressure on our balance of payments position, we must give special attention to the modernization of our plant and equipment. Forced to reconstruct after wartime devastation, our friends abroad now possess a modern industrial system helping to make them formidable competitors in world markets. If our own goods are to compete with foreign goods in price and quality, both at home and abroad, we shall need the most efficient plant and equipment.

At the same time, to meet the needs of a growing population and labor force, and to achieve a rising per capita income and employment level, we need a high and rising level of both private and public capital formation. . . .

High capital formation can be sustained only by a high and rising level of demand for goods and services. Indeed, the investment incentive itself can contribute materially to achieving the prosperous economy under which this incentive will make its maximum contribution to economic growth. . . .

Additional expenditures on plant and equipment will immediately create more jobs in the construction, lumber, steel, cement, machinery and other related capital-goods industries.

The staffing of these new plants, and filling the orders for new export markets, will require additional employees. The additional wages of these workers will help create still more jobs in consumer goods and service industries. The increase in jobs resulting from a full year's operation of such an incentive is estimated at about half a million. . . .

Elsewhere in the message the President recommended:

1. Elimination of tax-deferral privileges in developed countries, and "tax haven" deferral privileges in all countries.

2. Taxation of income from foreign investment companies in the same way as income from domestic investment companies.

3. Limiting or eliminating altogether the tax exemption on earned income enjoyed by Americans living abroad; and terminating the exemption from estate taxes of real property situated abroad.

4. Elimination of the double allowance for foreign income taxes on dividends.

5. A tax credit to businesses undertaking new plant and equipment investment expenditures.

6. Introduction of tax withholding on dividends and interest.

7. Repeal of the partial tax exemption that dividends have had since 1954.

8. Legislation to correct present abuses in the use of expense accounts.

9. Taxing, as income, of gains on sale of depreciable business property.

10. Remedial legislation covering taxes on co-operatives and certain financial institutions.

11. A variety of measures to improve tax administration, including a system of identifying all taxpayers by account numbers. By the time Congress adjourned, this last request was the only one to have won Congressional approval.

CONFLICTS OF INTEREST

Conflicts of interest are inevitable in human affairs, and government can never hope to be wholly free of them. Perhaps those in recent years had been no more frequent nor shocking than one might expect. But two considerations suggested that the time was ripe for a fundamental re-examination of the whole question: (1) statutes now on the books were clearly inadequate to handle certain problems that are a familiar part of modern government; and (2) the present statutes served in some instances to penalize good people and to keep valuable men from making their contribution to government.

In a special message to Congress on April 27, the President set forth his recommendations on this difficult question.

Special Message on Conflicts of Interest,
April 27, 1961

No responsibility of government is more fundamental than the responsibility of maintaining the highest standards of ethical behavior by those who conduct the public business. There can be no dissent from the principle that all officials must act with unwavering integrity, absolute impartiality and complete de-

votion to the public interest. This principle must be followed
not only in reality but in appearance. For the basis of effective
government is public confidence, and that confidence is endangered when ethical standards falter or appear to falter.

I have firm confidence in the integrity and dedication of
those who work for our government. Venal conduct by public
officials in this country has been comparatively rare, and the
few instances of official impropriety that have been uncovered
have usually not suggested any widespread departure from high
standards of ethics and moral conduct.

Nevertheless, in the past two decades, incidents have occurred to remind us that the laws and regulations governing
ethics in government are not adequate to the changed role of
the Federal Government, or to the changing conditions of our
society. In addition, many of the ethical problems confronting our public servants have become so complex as to defy
easy, common-sense solutions on the part of men of good will
seeking to observe the highest standards of conduct, and solutions have been hindered by lack of general regulatory guidelines. As a result many thoughtful observers have expressed
concern about the moral tone of government, and about the
need to restate basic principles in their application to contemporary facts.

Of course, public officials are not a group apart. They inevitably reflect the moral tone of the society in which they
live. And if that moral tone is injured—by fixed athletic con-
tests or television quiz shows, by widespread business con-
spiracies to fix prices, by the collusion of businessmen and
unions with organized crime, by cheating on expense accounts,
by the ignoring of traffic laws, or by petty tax evasion—then
the conduct of our government must be affected. Inevitably,

the moral standards of a society influence the conduct of all who live within it, the governed and those who govern.

The ultimate answer to ethical problems in government is honest people in a good ethical environment. No web of statute or regulation, however intricately conceived, can hope to deal with the myriad possible challenges to a man's integrity or his devotion to the public interest. Nevertheless, formal regulation is required, regulation which can lay down clear guidelines of policy, punish venality and double-dealing, and set a general ethical tone for the conduct of public business.

Such regulation, while setting the highest moral standards, must not impair the ability of the government to recruit personnel of the highest quality and capacity. Today's government needs men and women with a broad range of experience, knowledge and ability. It needs increasing numbers of people with top-flight executive talent. It needs hundreds of occasional and intermittent consultants and part-time experts to help deal with problems of increasing complexity and technical difficulty. In short, we need to draw upon America's entire reservoir of talent and skill to help conduct our generation's most important business, the public business.

This need to tap America's human resources for public purposes has blurred the distinctions between public and private life. It has led to a constant flow of people in and out of business, academic life and government. It has required us to contract with private institutions and call upon part-time consultants for important public work. It has resulted in a rapid rate of turnover among career government employees, as high as 20 per cent a year. And, as a result, it has gravely multiplied the risk of conflicts of interest while seriously complicating the problem of maintaining ethical standards. . . .

STATUTORY REFORM

There are seven statutes of general application termed "conflict-of-interest" statutes. Many others deal with particular
offices or very limited categories of employees. These latter
usually exempt officials from some or all of the general restrictions. Occasionally they impose additional obligations.

The seven statutes cover four basic problems:

1. The government employee who acts on behalf of the
government in a business transaction with an entity in which
he has a personal economic stake (18 U.S.C. 434).

2. The government employee who acts for an outside interest in certain dealings with the government (18 U.S.C. 216,
281, 283).

3. The government employee who receives compensation
from a private source for his government work (18 U.S.C.
1914).

4. The former government employee who acts in a representative capacity in certain transactions with the government
during a two-year period after the termination of his government service (18 U.S.C. 284, 5 U.S.C. 99).

Five of these statutes were enacted before 1873. Each was
enacted without co-ordination with any of the others. No two
of them use uniform terminology. All but one impose criminal
penalties. There is both overlap and inconsistency. Every study
of these laws has concluded that, while sound in principle,
they are grossly deficient in form and substance.

The fundamental defect of these statutes as presently written
is that, on the one hand, they permit an astonishing range
of private interests and activities by public officials which are
wholly incompatible with the duties of public office; on the

other hand, they create wholly unnecessary obstacles to re-cruiting qualified people for government service. . . .

Where some of these conflict-of-interest statutes are re-stricted to "claims of money and property," as the courts have said, they do not protect the government against the use of official position, influence or inside information to aid private individuals or organizations in government proceedings which involve no claims for money or property. Yet the danger of abuses of government position exists to an equal if not greater degree in proceedings such as license applications for TV or radio stations, airline routes, electric power sites, and similar requests for government aid, assistance or approval.

Thus, literally read, it would be a crime punishable by fine or imprisonment under these statutes for a postal clerk to assist his mother in filing a routine claim for a tax refund, but it would be permissible for a Cabinet officer to seek to influence an independent agency to award a license for a valuable TV station to a business associate in a venture where he shared the profits. . . .

Similar defects exist in the case of the government official who has left government service. Clearly such an official should be prohibited from resigning his position and "switching sides" in a matter which was before him in his official capacity. But for technical reasons the statutes aimed at this situation do not always hit the mark. There is nothing in the criminal statutes which would prevent the general counsel of the Fed-eral Power Commission from resigning to represent an unsuc-cessful license applicant who is contesting the Commission's decision in the courts (although such conduct might be grounds for disbarment). And a Commission employee who was not a lawyer could, in the present state of the law, unscrupulously benefit in such a case from his "inside information" without fear of sanctions.

But if the statutes often leave important areas unregulated, they also often serve as a bar to securing important personal services for the government through excessive regulation when no ethical problem really exists. Fundamentally, this is because the statutes fail to take into account the role in our government of the part-time or intermittent adviser whose counsel has become essential but who cannot afford to be deprived of private benefits, or reasonably requested to deprive himself, in the way now required by these laws. Wherever the government seeks the assistance of a highly skilled technician, be he scientist, accountant, lawyer or economist, such problems are encountered.

In general, these difficulties stem from the fact that even occasional consultants can technically be regarded as either "officers or employees" of the government, whether or not compensated. If so, they are all within the prohibitions applicable to regular full-time personnel. . . .

In the remaining sections of the message, the President:

1. Said that he would send to Congress a bill to accomplish a comprehensive revision of existing conflict-of-interest statutes, and to correct the difficulties and inconsistencies described above.

2. Called for legislation requiring each agency to establish a code of behavior governing ex parte *communication (i.e., undisclosed, informal contact between an agency official and a party interested in a matter before that official).*

3. Said that he would issue regulations: (a) limiting the

acceptance of gifts by government employees; *(b)* prohibiting government employees from using, for private gain, official information not available to the public; *(c)* directing that no government employee use his position to induce another individual to provide him with anything of economic value; and *(d)* directing that no government employee engage in outside employment "incompatible" with his government employment.

4. Announced that he would establish government-wide regulations controlling the continuance of property holdings by appointees to the Executive Branch.

5. Announced that he was designating in the Executive Office of the President a single officer to co-ordinate matters of governmental ethics.

The message concluded as follows:

Ultimately, high ethical standards can be maintained only if the leaders of government provide a personal example of dedication to the public service, and exercise their leadership to develop in all government employees an increasing sensitivity to the ethical and moral conditions imposed by public service. . . .

I realize, too, that perhaps the gravest responsibility of all rests upon the office of the President. No President can excuse or pardon the slightest deviation from irreproachable standards of behavior on the part of any member of the Executive Branch. For his firmness and determination is the ultimate source of public confidence in the government of the United States. And there is no consideration that can justify the undermining of that confidence.

CHAPTER VIII
THE LAND AND ITS WEALTH

"ABUNDANT PRODUCTION HAS FILLED OUR BINS AND WAREHOUSES, BUT ONE OUT OF TEN AMERICAN HOUSEHOLDS HAS A DIET SO INADEQUATE THAT IT FALLS BELOW TWO-THIRDS OF THE STANDARD NUTRITION REQUIREMENTS."

"AMERICAN AGRICULTURAL ABUNDANCE CAN BE FORGED INTO BOTH A SIGNIFICANT INSTRUMENT OF FOREIGN POLICY AND A WEAPON AGAINST DOMESTIC HARDSHIP AND HUNGER."

". . . IT IS OUR TASK IN OUR TIME AND IN OUR GENERATION TO HAND DOWN UNDIMINISHED TO THOSE WHO COME AFTER US, AS WAS HANDED DOWN TO US BY THOSE WHO WENT BEFORE, THE NATURAL WEALTH AND BEAUTY WHICH IS OURS."

On March 16 the President sent to the Congress his Message on Agriculture.

AGRICULTURE

Message to the Congress on Agriculture,
March 16, 1961

. . . As the provider of our food and fiber, American agriculture is a highly successful and highly efficient industry. In no other country, and at no other time in the history of our own farm economy, have so many people been so well provided with such abundance and variety at such low real cost. . . .

In short, our farmers deserve praise, not condemnation; and their efficiency should be a cause for gratitude, not something for which they are penalized. For their very efficiency and productivity lies at the heart of the distress in American agriculture. . . . Farming remains our largest industry. It employs twelve times as many people as work in steel and nine times as many as in the automobile industry. It employs, in fact, more people than steel, automobiles, public utilities and the transportation industry combined. The farmer is a consumer as well as a producer, and other economic groups are affected by the continued drop in farm purchasing power. Some $40 billion are spent each year for production goods and services needed on our farms and for the consumer goods used by farm families. Six million people are employed in the manufacture and distribution of the supplies that farmers use. Each year farm families spend from $2.5 to $3 billion for new automobiles, trucks, tractors and other farm machinery; and $3.5 billion for fuel, lubricants and maintenance of motor vehicles and machinery. It is deeply in the interest of all Americans that our agriculture be not only progressive but prosperous.

Yet as our farm families enter the 1960's, their incomes are lower relative to the rest of our population than at any time since the 1930's. Although there has been a continuous rise in consumer prices during the past ten years, farm income has steadily declined. Abundant production has filled our bins and warehouses, but one out of ten American households has a diet so inadequate that it falls below two-thirds of the standard nutrition requirements.

These paradoxes are of concern to all of us: the farmer, the taxpayer and the consumer. They affect the vitality of our nation, the strength of our most basic industry, agriculture, and the economic health of every community in the land.

Much of the current problem results from four factors:

First: The inability of millions of separate producers to control either output or price of their products. Acting individually the farmer can neither plan his production to meet modern requirements, and shift away from commodities for which there is limited demand, nor bargain effectively for a fair return.

Second: A technological revolution in agricultural production, which is still under way, that has resulted in generally increased yield from a reduced input of acreage and manpower, so that today each farmer produces the food and fiber necessary for twenty-five people, while at the turn of the century each farmer produced the food and fiber for only seven people.

Third: A faulty system of distribution, which allows one-half of the people of the free world to suffer from malnutrition at the very same time our surpluses have reached a point where the availability of adequate storage facilities has become a real problem.

Fourth: The steady and continued increase in farm costs. The average farm requires an investment of $36,000. The farmer's interest costs have increased over 300 per cent in the past decade. His equipment costs have increased 75 per cent.

The solution lies not so much in severe restriction upon our talent to produce as upon proper channeling of our abundance into more effective and expanded uses. American agricultural abundance can be forged into both a significant instrument of foreign policy and a weapon against domestic hardship and hunger. It is no less our purpose to insure that the farm family that produced this wealth will have a parity in income and equality in opportunity with urban families, for the family farm should be protected and preserved as a basic American institution.

Our intention is to accomplish these goals while eventually reducing the cost of our programs to the taxpayer. This can be accomplished in part because it is cheaper to use our agricultural products than to store them. Present storage costs total over $500 million a year, or $1.4 million every day.

But it must also be our purpose to see that farm products return a fair income because they are fairly priced. No farm program should exploit the consumer. But neither can it subsidize the consumer at the cost of subnormal incomes to the farmer. We cannot tolerate substandard conditions on the farm any more than we can in industry. A fair return is a necessity for labor, capital and management in industry. It is equally necessary for those who produce our food and fiber.

It must be our purpose to provide an agricultural program that will eventually eliminate the vast farm surpluses that overhang the market and overburden the economy; that will permit effective economies of administration; that will recognize the right of the consumer to fair prices; and that will permit the farmer to receive a fair return for his labor. . . .

In the remainder of the message, the President:

1. Asked for legislation to extend and increase the authority of the Secretary of Agriculture in the management of farm supply and the stabilization of farm income.

2. Proposed administrative and legislative measures to improve and expand the distribution and sale of agricultural products (including surplus) at home and abroad.

3. Recommended legislation "to reaffirm and protect the right of farmers to act together through their co-operatives in the processing and marketing of their products, the purchasing of supplies, and the furnishing of necessary services."

4. Urged passage of the Area Redevelopment Bill to aid those regions where farms are predominantly in the lowest income group.

5. Announced that he would liberalize and extend the lending operations of the Farm Home Administration, initiate measures to encourage storage of grain on the farm, and reinvigorate the rural electrification program.

6. Proposed administrative and legislative measures to improve privately owned woodlands as well as the national forests.

7. Asked Congress for funds to accelerate the program of the Soil Conservation Service.

On August 8, the President signed the Agricultural Act of 1961, which gave him a large part of what he asked for. But Congress refused to authorize the Secretary of Agriculture to draw up commodity stabilization programs which would be subject only to Congressional veto.

NATURAL RESOURCES

The President came to office with some firm ideas on the subject of natural resources—ideas which he expressed eloquently on more than one occasion. Perhaps his most vivid comments on the general subject are to be found in a few paragraphs from a speech at the dedication of the National Wildlife Federation Building.

Remarks at the Dedication Ceremonies of the National Wildlife Federation Building, March 3, 1961

. . . At the Inauguration, Robert Frost read a poem which began, "The land was ours before we were the land's," meaning, in part, that this new land of ours sustained us before we were a nation. And although we are now the land's, a nation of people matched to a continent, we still draw our strength and sustenance in this city and in every other city across our country from the earth.

Throughout our history our soil and water, our forests and minerals, have provided the resources upon which this country grew; and our power ascended. Today, this great gift of material wealth provides the foundation upon which the defense of freedom rests, here and around the world. And our future greatness and our strength depend upon the continued abundant use of our natural resources.

Thus it is our task in our time and in our generation to

hand down undiminished to those who come after us, as was handed down to us by those who went before, the natural wealth and beauty which is ours. . . .

No governmental program will be effective, our resources will not be protected, without the concern and hope of every private citizen. By mobilizing private effort through your organization you are helping not only to develop the wildlife resources of our country, but you are helping to create the kind of America that is our common goal: an America of open spaces, of fresh water and green country, a place where wildlife and natural beauty cannot be despoiled, where an increasingly urbanized population can still go to the country, can still turn back the clock of our civilization and find the material and spiritual strength upon which our greatness as a country depends. . . .

But the President's major systematic pronouncement on the subject came in his Special Message on Natural Resources:

Special Message on Natural Resources,
February 23, 1961

From the beginning of civilization, every nation's basic wealth and progress has stemmed in large measure from its natural resources. This nation has been, and is now, especially fortunate in the blessings we have inherited. Our entire society rests upon, and is dependent upon, our water, our land, our forests and our minerals. How we use these resources influences our health, security, economy and well-being.

But if we fail to chart a proper course of conservation and

development, if we fail to use these blessings prudently, we will be in trouble within a short time. In the resource field, predictions of future use have been consistently understated. But even under conservative projections, we face a future of critical shortages and handicaps. By the year 2000, a United States population of 300 million, nearly doubled in forty years, will need far greater supplies of farm products, timber, water, minerals, fuels, energy and opportunities for outdoor recreation. Present projections tell us that our water use will double in the next twenty years; that we are harvesting our supply of high-grade timber more rapidly than the development of new growth; that too much of our fertile topsoil is being washed away; that our minerals are being exhausted at increasing rates; and that the nation's remaining undeveloped areas of great natural beauty are being rapidly pre-empted for other uses.

Wise investment in a resource program today will return vast dividends tomorrow, and failures to act now may be opportunities lost forever. Our country has been generous with us in this regard, and we cannot now ignore her needs for future development.

This is not a matter of concern for only one section of the country. All those who fish and hunt, who build industrial centers, who need electricity to light their homes and lighten their burdens, who require water for home, industrial, and recreational purposes—in short, every citizen in every state of the Union—all have a stake in a sound resources program. . . .

WATER RESOURCES

Our nation has been blessed with a bountiful supply of water; but it is not a blessing we can regard with complacency. We now use over 300 billion gallons of water a day, much of it wastefully. By 1980 we will need 600 billion gallons a day.

Our supply of water is not always consistent with our needs of time and place. Floods one day in one section may be countered in other days or in other sections by the severe water shortages which are now afflicting many Eastern urban areas and are particularly critical in the West. Our available water supply must be used to give maximum benefits for all purposes —hydroelectric power, irrigation and reclamation, navigation, recreation, health, home and industry. If all areas of the country are to enjoy a balanced growth, our Federal reclamation and other water resource programs will have to give increased attention to municipal and industrial water and power supplies as well as irrigation and land redemption. . . .

Pollution of our country's rivers and streams has, as a result of our rapid population and industrial growth and change, reached alarming proportions. To meet all needs—domestic, agricultural, industrial, recreational—we shall have to use and reuse the same water, maintaining quality as well as quantity. In many areas of the country we need new sources of supply, but in all areas we must protect the supplies we have. . . .

No water resources program is of greater long-range importance, for relief not only of our shortages, but for arid nations the world over, than our efforts to find an effective and economical way to convert water from the world's greatest, cheapest natural resources, our oceans, into water fit for consumption in the home and by industry. Such a breakthrough would end bitter struggles between neighbors, states and nations, and bring new hope for millions who live out their lives in dire shortage of usable water and all its physical and economic blessings, though living on the edge of a great body of water throughout a parched lifetime.

This Administration is currently engaged in redoubled efforts to select the most promising approaches to economical desalinization of ocean and brackish waters, and then focus our energies more intensively on those approaches. . . .

I now pledge that, when this know-how is achieved, it will immediately be made available to every nation in the world who wishes it, along with appropriate technical and other assistance for its use. Indeed, the United States welcomes now the co-operation of all other nations who wish to join in this effort at present. . . .

ELECTRIC POWER

To keep pace with the growth of our economy and national defense requirements, expansion of this nation's power facilities will require intensive effort by all segments of our power industry. Through 1980, according to present estimates of the Federal Power Commission, total installed capacity should triple if we are to meet our nation's need for essential economic growth. Sustained heavy expansion by all power suppliers, public, co-operative and private, is clearly needed.

The role of the Federal Government in supplying an important segment of this power is now long established and must continue. We will meet our responsibilities in this field. . . .

Our efforts to achieve economically competitive nuclear power before the end of this decade in areas where fossil fuel costs are high will be encouraged through basic research, engineering developments and construction of various prototype and full-scale reactors by the Atomic Energy Commission in co-operation with industry. . . .

To deal with these and related problems, the President:

1. Announced that he would establish a Presidential Advisory Committee on Natural Resources, and would request the National Academy of Sciences to evaluate the state of research on conservation, development and use of natural resources.

2. Announced that he was rejecting a "no new starts" policy on water-resources and flood-control projects, and was requesting appropriate department and agency heads to schedule an orderly program of such projects.

3. Asked Congress to authorize the establishment of planning commissions with a view to developing comprehensive river-basin plans by 1970; urged legislation permitting the reservation of known future reservoir sites; and asked the Senate to approve the Columbia River Joint Development Treaty with Canada.

4. Promised acceleration of the government's flood-control program, and asked for a re-evaluation of the soil-conservation and watershed-management programs.

5. Proposed various legislative and administrative measures to accelerate water-pollution control, and urged an effective Federal program of air-pollution control.

6. Urged Congress to extend and increase support for the current saline water conversion research program.

7. Announced the principles to be followed in marketing Federal power, and directed the Secretary of the Interior "to develop plans for the early interconnection of areas served by that Department's marketing agencies with adequate common carrier transmission lines; to plan for further national co-operative pooling of electric power, both public and private; and to enlarge such pooling as now exists. . . ."

8. Urged Congress to accelerate forest development on Federal public lands; announced an intensified program of building approved access roads to public forests; and announced measures to improve management, usage and conservation of public-domain lands.

9. Stated that he would send to Congress a national program for oceanography.

10. Proposed administrative and legislative measures for wilderness protection, establishment of additional Federally owned recreational areas, and expansion of fish- and wildlife-conservation programs.

Of the proposed natural resources legislation, Congress authorized grants to help communities build sewage treatment plants, increased the amount of matching grants to states for water pollution control, and passed a modified version of the Administration's saline water conversion program. Also, the Senate ratified the Columbia River Joint Development Treaty with Canada. An Administration bill concerned with protection of wilderness areas was passed by the Senate but was not acted upon in the House. A bill to establish the Cape Cod National Seashore Park was signed by the President on August 7.

CHAPTER IX
CONCERN FOR THE INDIVIDUAL

"THE HUMAN MIND IS OUR FUNDAMENTAL RESOURCE."

"I HAVE TRIED TO MAKE THE WHOLE TONE AND THRUST OF THIS OFFICE AND THIS ADMINISTRATION ONE THAT WILL DEMAND A HIGHER STANDARD OF EXCELLENCE FROM EVERY INDIVIDUAL. . . ."

"IN ACCORDANCE WITH THE CLEAR PROHIBITION OF THE CONSTITUTION, NO ELEMENTARY OR SECONDARY SCHOOL FUNDS ARE ALLOCATED FOR CONSTRUCTING CHURCH SCHOOLS OR PAYING CHURCH SCHOOL TEACHERS' SALARIES. . . ."

"THE HEALTH OF OUR NATION IS A KEY TO ITS FUTURE."

President Kennedy's keen interest in education is familiar to all who have followed his career. On February 20 he sent to Congress his Special Message on Education.

EDUCATION

Special Message to the Congress on Education,
February 20, 1961

Our progress as a nation can be no swifter than our progress in education. Our requirements for world leadership, our hopes for economic growth, and the demands of citizenship itself in an era such as this all require the maximum development of every young American's capacity.

The human mind is our fundamental resource. A balanced Federal program must go well beyond incentives for investment in plant and equipment. It must include equally determined measures to invest in human beings, both in their basic education and training and in their more advanced preparation for professional work. Without such measures, the Federal Government will not be carrying out its responsibilities for expanding the base of our economic and military strength. . . .

Education must remain a matter of state and local control, and higher education a matter of individual choice. But education is increasingly expensive. Too many state and local governments lack the resources to assure an adequate education for every child. Too many classrooms are overcrowded. Too many teachers are underpaid. Too many talented individuals cannot afford the benefits of higher education. Too many academic institutions cannot afford the cost of, or find room for, the growing numbers of students seeking admission in the sixties.

Our twin goals must be: a new standard of excellence in education, and the availability of such excellence to all who are willing and able to pursue it.

ASSISTANCE TO PUBLIC ELEMENTARY
AND SECONDARY SCHOOLS

. . . An average net gain of nearly one million pupils a year during the next ten years will overburden a school system already strained by well over a half-million pupils in curtailed or half-day sessions, a school system financed largely by a property tax incapable of bearing such an increased load in most communities.

But providing the quality and quantity of teachers and facilities to meet this demand will be major problems. Even today, there are some ninety thousand teachers who fall short of full certification standards. Tens of thousands of others must attempt to cope with classes of unwieldy size because there are insufficient teachers available.

We cannot obtain more and better teachers—and our children should have the best—unless steps are taken to increase teachers' salaries. At present salary levels, the classroom cannot compete in financial rewards with other professional work that requires similar academic background.

It is equally clear that we do not have enough classrooms. In order to meet current needs and accommodate increasing enrollments, if every child is to have the opportunity of a full-day education in an adequate classroom, a total of 600,000 classrooms must be constructed during the next ten years.

These problems are common to all states. They are particularly severe in those states which lack the financial resources to provide a better education, regardless of their own efforts. Additional difficulties, too often overlooked, are encountered in areas of special educational need, where economic or social circumstances impose special burdens and opportunities on the public school. These areas of special educational need include our depressed areas of chronic unemployment and the slum neighborhoods of our larger cities, where underprivileged children are overcrowded into substandard housing. . . . The proportion of drop-outs, delinquency and classroom disorders in such areas is alarmingly high.

I recommend to the Congress a three-year program of general Federal assistance for public elementary and secondary classroom construction and teachers' salaries.

Based essentially on the bill which passed the Senate last year (S.8), although beginning at a more modest level of expenditure, this program would assure every state of no less than $15 for every public school student in average daily attendance, with the total amount appropriated ($666 million being authorized in the first year, rising to $866 million over a three-year period) distributed according to the equalization formula contained in the last year's Senate bill, and already familiar to the Congress by virtue of its similarity to the formulas contained in the Hill-Burton Hospital Construction and other acts. Ten per cent of the funds allocated to each state in the first year, and an equal amount thereafter, is to be used to help meet the unique problems of each state's "areas of special educational need"—depressed areas, slum neighborhoods and others.

. . . In accordance with the clear prohibition of the Constitution, no elementary or secondary school funds are allocated for constructing church schools or paying church school teachers' salaries; and thus nonpublic school children are rightfully not counted in determining the funds each state will receive for its public schools. Each state will be expected to maintain its own effort or contribution; and every state whose effort is below the national average will be expected to increase that proportion of its income which is devoted to public elementary and secondary education. . . .

In the remainder of the message, the President:

1. Recommended that Congress extend the current College Housing Loan Program with a five-year $250-million-a-year program.

2. Recommended legislation establishing a new long-term, low-interest-rate loan program for academic facilities (classrooms, laboratories, libraries and related structures) and authorizing $300 million in loans each year for five years.

3. Announced that he would ask Congress to amend and expand the Student Loan and other provisions of the National Defense Education Act.

4. Recommended a five-year program of state-administered college scholarships for talented and needy students, beginning with 25,000 scholarships the first year and rising to 50,000 a year by the third, with "cost of education" supplements to the college the young person chooses to attend.

5. Announced that an advisory body would be appointed to review and re-evaluate the National Vocational Education Acts.

As everyone knows, the Administration's education bill provoked vigorous debate, not only in Congress but in the nation at large. The Church-State issue was brought into it when proponents of the parochial schools indicated that they would oppose the Administration bill unless Congress also passed a bill authorizing loans to non-public secondary schools. In

a press conference on March 1, the President commented on
the constitutionality of the latter measure.

Fifth Press Conference,
March 1, 1961

QUESTION: Mr. President . . . could you elaborate on why
you have not recommended Federal aid to . . . private and
parochial elementary and secondary schools?

THE PRESIDENT: Well, the Constitution clearly prohibits
aid to . . . the parochial school. There is no doubt about that.
The Everson case, which is probably the most celebrated case
. . . [dealt with the question of whether it was] possible for a
local community to provide bus rides for non-public school
children. . . . All through the majority and minority statements
on that particular question there was a very clear prohibition
against aid to the school direct. The Supreme Court made its
decision in the Everson case by determining that the aid was
to the child, not to the school. . . . There isn't any room for
debate on that subject. It is prohibited by the Constitution, and
the Supreme Court has made that very clear. Therefore,
there would be no possibility of our recommending it.

In the Everson case, to which the President referred, the
Supreme Court ruled that it is constitutional to use tax funds
for transportation of children to and from all non-profit
schools; but the Court emphasized that the constitutionality
of such payment rests on the fact that its purpose is public
safety and not private education.

The Administration's education bill was finally voted down. The New York Times *described it as the President's most conspicuous defeat at the hands of Congress. The President said: "... the need to improve the standards of education in this country will still be before the Congress next year."*

CIVIL RIGHTS

Meanwhile, in the Southern states an historic struggle was in progress—the effort to make the civil rights of the Negro a reality. And though bus stations became, in mid-1961, the most spectacular battleground of that struggle, the sector of deepest significance continued to be the schools.

Early in his Administration the President took note of the struggle in a telegram to a conference of the Civil Rights Commission in Williamsburg, Virginia.

Telegram,
February 2, 1961

Let me here pay tribute to ... the men and women responsible for maintaining our public schools and for carrying through the process of desegregation—principals, officers of school boards and public school teachers. The constitutional requirement of desegregation has presented them with many new responsibilities and hard challenges. In New Orleans today, as in many other places represented in your three conferences, these loyal citizens and educators are meeting these responsibilities and challenges with quiet intelligence and true courage.

The whole country is in their debt, for our public school system must be preserved and improved. Our very survival as a free nation depends upon it. This is no time for schools to close for any reason, and certainly no time for schools to be closed in the name of racial discrimination. If we are to give the leadership the world requires of us, we must be true to the great principles of our Constitution, the very principles which distinguish us from our adversaries in the world.

Let me also pay tribute to the school children and their parents, of both races, who have been on the front lines of this problem. In accepting the command of the Constitution with dignity they too are contributing to the education of all Americans.

In September Congress extended the life of the Civil Rights Commission for another two years.

HEALTH

The President's program in the field of health is outlined in the message which he sent to Congress on February 9, portions of which follow.

Special Message to the Congress on Health and Hospital Care, February 9, 1961

The health of our nation is a key to its future—to its economic vitality, to the morale and efficiency of its citizens, to our success in achieving our own goals and demonstrating to others the benefits of a free society. . . . This is a matter of national concern.

More than $25 billion a year, over 6 per cent of our national income, is being spent from public and private funds for health services. Yet there are major deficiencies in the quality and distribution of these services.

The dramatic results of new medicines and new methods, opening the way to a fuller and more useful life, are too often beyond the reach of those who need them most.

Financial inability, absence of community resources and shortages of trained personnel keep too many people from getting what medical knowledge can obtain for them.

Those among us who are over sixty-five, sixteen million today in the United States, go to the hospital more often and stay longer than their younger neighbors. Their physical activity is limited by six times as much disability as the rest of the population. Their annual medical bill is twice that of persons under sixty-five, but their annual income is only half as high.

The nation's children, now 40 per cent of our population, have urgent needs which must be met. Many still die in infancy. Many are not immunized against diseases which can be prevented, have inadequate diets or unnecessarily endure physical and emotional problems.

These and other problems of health care can and must be met. Only a part of the responsibility rests with the Federal Government. But its powers and resources make its role essential in four areas for improving health care: social insurance, facilities, personnel and research.

HEALTH INSURANCE FOR THE AGED

Twenty-six years ago this nation adopted the principle that every member of the labor force and his family should be insured against the haunting fear of loss of income caused by retirement, death or unemployment. To that we have added insurance against the economic loss caused by disability.

But there remains a significant gap that denies to all but those with the highest incomes a full measure of security: the high cost of ill health in old age. One out of five aged couples drawing Social Security benefits must go to the hospital each year. Half of those going to hospitals incur bills in excess of $700 a year. This is over one-third of the total annual income of a typical couple, more than a modest food budget for an entire year. Many simply do not obtain and cannot afford the care they need.

The measure adopted by the Congress last year recognized the problem of those needy aged requiring welfare assistance to meet their medical costs. But now we must meet the needs of those millions who have no wish to receive care at the taxpayers' expense, but who are nevertheless staggered by the drain on their savings, or those of their children, caused by an extended hospital stay.

In our Social Security and Railroad Retirement systems we have the instruments which can spread the cost of health services in old age over the working years, effectively, and in a manner consistent with the dignity of the individual. By using these proved systems to provide health insurance protection, it will be possible for our older people to get the vital hospital services they need without exhausting their resources or turning to public assistance. The self-supporting insurance method of financing the cost of such health services is certainly to be preferred to an expansion of public assistance, and should reduce the number of those needing medical care under the public assistance program. The state and local money thus freed should be further used to help provide services not included in this proposal, and to assist those not covered.

For it should be stressed that this is a very modest proposal cut to meet absolutely essential needs, and with sufficient "deductible" requirements to discourage any malingering or unnecessary overcrowding of our hospitals.

In essence, I am recommending enactment of a health insurance program under the Social Security System that will provide the following benefits:

First, in-patient hospital services up to 90 days in a single spell of illness, for all costs in excess of $10 per day for the first 9 days (with a minimum of $20), and full costs for the remaining 81 days. Because hospital costs place by far the heaviest and most unmanageable burden on older persons, it is these services that should receive major emphasis in any health insurance program.

Second, skilled nursing home services up to 180 days immediately after discharge from a hospital. To provide an incentive for use of these less expensive facilities, an individual could, in short, receive two days of skilled nursing home care in place of one day of hospital care when this satisfies his requirements.

Third, hospital out-patient clinic diagnostic services for all costs in excess of $20. These services, too, will reduce the need for hospital admissions and encourage early diagnosis.

Fourth, community visiting-nurse services, and related home health services, for a limited period of time. These will enable many older people to receive proper health care in their own homes.

I propose that these insurance benefits be available to all persons aged sixty-five and over who are eligible for Social Security or Railroad Retirement benefits.

This program would be financed by an increase in Social Security contributions of one-quarter of one per cent each on employers and employees, and by an increase in the maximum earnings base from $4,800 a year to $5,000, which would amply cover the cost of all insurance benefits provided. The system would be self-supporting and would not place any burden on the general revenues.

This program is not a program of socialized medicine. It is a program of prepayment of health costs with absolute freedom of choice guaranteed. Every person will choose his own doctor and hospital.

No service performed by any physician at either home or office, and no fee he charges for such services, would be involved, covered or affected in any way. There would be no supervision or control over the practice of medicine by any doctor or over the manner in which medical services are provided by any hospital. The program is a sound one and entirely in accordance with the traditional American system of placing responsibility on the employee and the employer, rather than on the general taxpayer, to help finance retirement and health costs. . . .

In the remainder of the message, the President recommended:
1. Federal scholarships for medical and dental students, and cost-of-education grants to the schools they attend.

2. Matching grants for construction, expansion or restoration of medical and dental schools to increase their capacities.

3. Funds for construction of nursing homes and for the improvement of nursing home and home-nursing services.

4. Increased funds for medical research and construction grants for medical research facilities and experimental or demonstration hospitals.

5. Establishment of a National Institute of Child Health and Human Development; and increased appropriations for the Maternal and Child Health, Crippled Children, and Child Welfare programs of the Children's Bureau.

6. Accelerated programs in youth fitness and vocational rehabilitation.

In October the Congress passed the Community Health Services and Facilities Act of 1961, which authorized Federal aid for development of outpatient services, construction of research facilities, research on hospital design, construction of nursing homes and for state and local public-health services. But the President's program of health insurance for the aged awaited Congressional action in 1962.

In April a British journalist, Mr. Ian Trethowan, commented on the fact that the President's programs in this field seemed to be "running into a certain amount of opposition." The President replied: "Well, any time you try to do anything, there are a lot of people who like it the way it used to be."

CHAPTER X
STRENGTHENING THE FREE WORLD

"THE FUNDAMENTAL TASK OF OUR FOREIGN-AID PROGRAM . . . IS TO HELP MAKE AN HISTORICAL DEMONSTRATION THAT . . . ECONOMIC GROWTH AND POLITICAL DEMOCRACY CAN DEVELOP HAND IN HAND."

". . . NO AMOUNT OF ARMS . . . CAN HELP STABILIZE THOSE GOVERNMENTS WHICH ARE UNABLE OR UNWILLING TO ACHIEVE SOCIAL AND ECONOMIC REFORM AND DEVELOPMENT. . . . THE MOST SKILLFUL COUNTER-GUERRILLA EFFORTS CANNOT SUCCEED WHERE THE LOCAL POPULATION IS TOO CAUGHT UP IN ITS OWN MISERY TO BE CONCERNED ABOUT THE ADVANCE OF COMMUNISM."

". . . THERE IS NO POINT IN SPEAKING OUT AGAINST THE SPREAD OF COMMUNISM IF WE ARE UNWILLING TO RECOGNIZE WHICH WEAPONS ARE MOST NEEDED IN THAT STRUGGLE. THERE IS NO POINT IN CALLING FOR VIGOROUS ACTION TO PROTECT OUR SECURITY IF WE ARE UNWILLING TO PAY THE PRICE. . . ."

On no other issue of foreign or domestic affairs did the new Administration bring to bear more vigor and imagination than on foreign aid. Following are excerpts from the special message on that subject which the President sent to the Congress in March.

FOREIGN AID

Special Message to the Congress on Foreign Aid,
March 22, 1961

This nation must begin any discussion of "foreign aid" in 1961 with the recognition of three facts:

1. Existing foreign aid programs and concepts are largely unsatisfactory and unsuited for our needs and for the needs of the underdeveloped world as it enters the sixties.

2. The economic collapse of those free but less developed nations which now stand poised between sustained growth and economic chaos would be disastrous to our national security, harmful to our comparative prosperity and offensive to our conscience.

3. There exists, in the 1960's, an historic opportunity for a major economic assistance effort by the free industrialized nations to move more than half the people of the less-developed nations into self-sustained economic growth, while the rest move substantially closer to the day when they, too, will no longer have to depend on outside assistance.

I

Foreign aid, America's unprecedented response to world challenge, has not been the work of one party or one Administration. It has moved forward under the leadership of two great Presidents, Harry Truman and Dwight Eisenhower, and drawn its support from forward-looking members of both political parties in the Congress and throughout the nation.

Our first major foreign aid effort was an emergency program of relief, of food and clothing and shelter, to areas devastated by World War II. Next we embarked on the Marshall Plan, a towering and successful program to rebuild the economies of Western Europe and prevent a Communist takeover. This was followed by Point Four, an effort to make scientific and technological advances available to the people of developing nations. And recently the concept of development assistance, coupled with the Organization for Economic Co-operation and Development, has opened the door to a united free world effort to assist the economic and social development of the less-developed areas of the world.

To achieve this new goal we will need to renew the spirit of common effort which lay behind our past efforts. We must also revise our foreign aid organization, and our basic concepts of operation to meet the new problems which now confront us.

For no objective supporter of foreign aid can be satisfied with the existing program, actually a multiplicity of programs. Bureaucratically fragmented, awkward and slow, its administration is diffused over a haphazard and irrational structure covering at least four departments and several other agencies. The program is based on a series of legislative measures and administrative procedures conceived at different times and for different purposes, many of them now obsolete, inconsistent and unduly rigid and thus unsuited for our present needs and purposes. Its weaknesses have begun to undermine confidence in our effort both here and abroad.

The program requires a highly professional skilled service, attracting substantial members of high-caliber men and women capable of sensitive dealing with other governments, and with a deep understanding of the process of economic development.

However, uncertainty and declining public prestige have both contributed to a fall in the morale and efficiency of those employees in the field, who are repeatedly frustrated by the delays and confusions caused by overlapping agency jurisdictions and unclear objectives. Only the persistent efforts of those dedicated and hard-working public servants who have kept the program going managed to bring some success to our efforts overseas.

In addition, uneven and undependable short-term financing has weakened the incentive for the long-term planning and self-help by the recipient nations which are essential to serious economic development. The lack of stability and continuity in the program, the necessity to accommodate all planning to a yearly deadline, when combined with a confusing multiplicity of American aid agencies within a single nation abroad, have reduced the effectiveness of our own assistance and made more difficult the task of setting realistic targets and sound standards. Piecemeal projects, hastily designed to match the rhythm of the fiscal year, are no substitute for orderly long-term planning. The ability to make long-range commitments has enabled the Soviet Union to use its aid program to make developing nations economically dependent on Russian support, thus advancing the aims of world Communism.

Although our aid programs have helped to avoid economic chaos and collapse and assisted many nations to maintain their independence and freedom, nevertheless it is a fact that many of the nations we are helping are not much nearer sustained economic growth than they were when our aid program began. Money spent to meet crisis situations or short-term political objectives, while helping to maintain national integrity and independence, has rarely moved the recipient nation toward greater economic stability. . . .

II

... widespread poverty and chaos lead to a collapse of existing political and social structures which would inevitably invite the advance of totalitarianism into every weak and unstable area. Thus our own security would be endangered and our prosperity imperiled. A program of assistance to the underdeveloped nations must continue because the nation's interest and the cause of political freedom require it.

We live at a very special moment in history. . . . Latin America, Africa, the Middle East and Asia are caught up in the adventures of asserting their independence and modernizing their old ways of life. These new nations need aid in loans and technical assistance just as we in the northern half of the world drew successively on one another's capital and know-how as we moved into industrialization and regular growth.

But in our time these new nations need help for a special reason. Without exception they are under Communist pressure. In many cases, that pressure is direct and military. In others, it takes the form of intense subversive activity designed to break down and supersede the new, and often frail, modern institutions they have thus far built.

But the fundamental task of our foreign aid program in the 1960's is not negatively to fight Communism. Its fundamental task is to help make an historical demonstration that in the twentieth century as in the nineteenth, in the southern half of the globe as in the north, economic growth and political democracy can develop hand in hand.

In short, we have not only obligations to fulfill; we have great opportunities to realize. We are, I am convinced, on the threshold of a truly united and major effort by the free industrialized nations to assist the less-developed nations on a long-term basis. Many of these less-developed nations are on the threshold of achieving sufficient economic, social and political strength and self-sustained growth to stand permanently on their own feet. The 1960's can be, and must be, the crucial "Decade of Development"; the period when many less-developed nations make the transition into self-sustained growth; the period in which an enlarged community of free, stable and self-reliant nations can reduce world tensions and insecurity. *This goal is in our grasp if, and only if, the other industrialized nations now join us in developing with the recipients a set of commonly agreed criteria, a set of long-range goals, and a common undertaking to meet those goals, in which each nation's contribution is related to the contributions of others and to the precise needs of each less-developed nation.* Our job, in its largest sense, is to create a new partnership between the northern and southern halves of the world, to which all free nations can contribute, in which each free nation must assume a responsibility proportional to its means.

We must unite the free industrialized nations in a common effort to help those nations within reach of stable growth get under way. And the foundation for this unity has already been laid by the creation of the Organization for Economic Co-operation and Development under the leadership of President Eisenhower. Such a unified effort will help launch the economies of the newly developing countries "into orbit," bringing them to a stage of self-sustained growth where extraordinary outside assistance is not required. If this can be done, and I have every reason to hope it can be done, then this decade will be a significant one indeed in the history of free men.

But our success in achieving these goals, in creating an environment in which the energies of struggling peoples can be devoted to constructive purposes in the world community, and our success in enlisting a greater common effort toward this end on the part of other industrialized nations, depends to a large extent upon the scope and continuity of our own efforts. If we encourage recipient countries to dramatize a series of short-term crises as a basis for our aid, instead of depending on a plan for long-term goals, then we will dissipate our funds, our good will and our leadership. Nor will we be any nearer either to our security goals or to the end of the foreign aid burden.

In short, this Congress at this session must make possible a dramatic turning point in the troubled history of foreign aid to the underdeveloped world. We must say to the less-developed nations, *if they are willing to undertake necessary internal reform and self-help,* and to the other industrialized nations, *if they are willing to undertake a much greater effort on a much broader scale,* that we then intend during this coming decade of development to achieve a decisive turn-around in the fate of the less-developed world, looking toward the ultimate day when all nations can be self-reliant and when foreign aid will no longer be needed. . . .

This will require leadership, by this country in this year. And it will require a fresh approach, a more logical, efficient and successful long-term plan, for American foreign aid. I strongly recommend to the Congress the enactment of such a plan, as contained in a measure to be sent shortly to the Congress and described below.

III

If our foreign aid funds are to be prudently and effectively used, we need a whole new set of basic concepts and principles:

1. Unified administration and operation—a single agency in Washington and the field, equipped with a flexible set of tools, in place of several competing and confusing aid units.

2. Country plans—a carefully thought-through program tailored to meet the needs and the resource potential of each individual country, instead of a series of individual, unrelated projects. Frequently, in the past, our development goals and projects have not been undertaken as integral steps in a long-range economic development program.

3. Long-term planning and financing, the only way to make meaningful and economical commitments.

4. Special emphasis on development loans repayable in dollars, more conducive to business-like relations and mutual respect than sustaining grants or loans repaid in local currencies, although some instances of the latter are unavoidable.

5. Special attention to those nations most willing and able to mobilize their own resources, make necessary social and economic reforms, engage in long-range planning, and make the other efforts necessary if these are to reach the stage of self-sustaining growth.

6. Multilateral approach—a program and level of commitments designed to encourage and complement an increased effort by other industrialized nations.

7. A new agency with new personnel, drawing upon the most competent and dedicated career servants now in the field, and attracting the highest quality from every part of the nation.

8. Separation from military assistance. Our program of aid to social and economic development must be seen on its own merits, and judged in the light of its vital and distinctive contribution to our basic security needs. . . .

IV

. . . At the center of the new effort must be national development programs. It is essential that the developing nations set for themselves sensible targets; that these targets be based on balanced programs for their own economic, educational and social growth, programs which use their own resources to the maximum. . . . Thus, the first requirement is that each recipient government seriously undertake to the best of its ability on its own those efforts of resource mobilization, self-help and internal reform, including land reform, tax reform and improved education and social justice, which its own development requires and which would increase its capacity to absorb external capital productivity. . . .

. . . It will be necessary, for the time being, to provide grant assistance to those nations that are hard-pressed by external or internal pressure, so that they can meet those pressures and maintain their independence. In such cases it will be our objective to help them, as soon as circumstances permit, make the transition from instability and stagnation to growth, shifting our assistance as rapidly as possible from a grant to a development loan basis. For our new program should not be based merely on reaction to Communist threats or short-term crises. We have a positive interest in helping less-developed nations provide decent living standards for their people and achieve sufficient strength, self-respect and independence to become self-reliant members of the community of nations. And thus our aid should be conditioned on the recipients' ability and willingness to take the steps necessary to reach that goal. . . .

V

A program based on long-range plans instead of short-run crises cannot be financed on a short-term basis. Long-term authorization, planning and financing are the key to the continuity and efficiency of the entire program. If we are unwilling to make such a long-term commitment, we cannot expect any increased response from other potential donors or any realistic planning from the recipient nations.

I recommend, therefore, an authorization for the new aid agency of not less than five years, with borrowing authority also for five years to commit and make dollar repayable loans within the limits spelled out below. No other step would be such a clear signal of our intentions to all the world. No other step would do more to help obtain the service of top-flight personnel. And in no other way can we encourage the less-developed nations to make a sustained national effort over a long-term period.

For, if we are to have a program designed to brighten the future, that program must have a future. Experience has shown that long-range needs cannot be met evenly and economically by a series of one-year programs. Close consultation and cooperation with the Congress and its committees will still be essential, including an annual review of the program. . . .

The President returned to the subject in his address to the nation on June 6 following his European trip. Recalling his conversations with the Soviet Premier, the President said:

Report to the Nation,
June 6, 1961

[Mr. Khrushchev] was certain that the tide was moving his way, that the revolution of rising peoples would eventually be a Communist revolution, and that the so-called wars of liberation . . . supported by the Kremlin, would replace the old methods of direct aggression and invasion.

In the 1940's and early 1950's, the great danger was from Communist armies marching across free borders, which we saw in Korea. Our nuclear monopoly helped to prevent this in other areas. Now we face a new and different threat. We no longer have a nuclear monopoly. Their missiles, they believe, will hold off our missiles, and their troops can match our troops should we intervene in these so-called wars of liberation. Thus, the local conflict they support can turn in their favor through guerrillas or insurgents or subversion.

A small group of disciplined Communists could exploit discontent and misery in a country where the average income may be sixty or seventy dollars a year and seize control, therefore, of an entire country without Communist troops ever crossing any international frontier. This is the Communist theory.

But I believe just as strongly that time will prove it wrong, that liberty and independence and self-determination, not Communism, is the future of man, and that free men have the will and the resources to win the struggle for freedom. But it is clear that this struggle in this area of the new and poorer nations will be a continuing crisis of this decade.

Mr. Khrushchev had one point which I wish to pass on. He said there are many disorders throughout the world, and he should not be blamed for them all. He is quite right. It is easy to dismiss as Communist-inspired every antigovernment or anti-American riot, every overthrow of a corrupt regime, or every mass protest against misery and despair. These are not all Communist-inspired. The Communists move in to exploit them, to infiltrate their leadership, to ride their crest to victory. But the Communists did not create the conditions which caused them.

In short, the hopes for freedom in these areas which see so much poverty and illiteracy, so many children who are sick, so many children who die in the first year, so many families without homes, so many families without hope—the future for freedom in these areas rests with the local people also and their governments.

If they have the will to determine their own future, if their governments have the support of their own people, if their honest and progressive measures helping their people have inspired confidence and zeal, then no guerrilla or insurgent action can succeed. But where those conditions do not exist, a military guarantee against external attack from across a border offers little protection against internal decay. . . .

We have an historic opportunity to help these countries build their societies until they are so strong and broadly based that only an outside invasion could topple them, and that threat, we know, can be stopped.

We can train and equip their forces to resist Communist-supplied insurrections. We can help develop the industrial and agricultural base on which new living standards can be built.

We can encourage better administration and better education and better tax and land distribution and a better life for the people. . . .

If we are not prepared to assist them in making a better life for their people, then I believe that the prospects for freedom in those areas are uncertain. . . . The burden is heavy and we have carried it for many years. But I believe that this fight is not over. This battle goes on, and we have to play our part in it. And therefore I hope again that we will assist these people so that they can remain free.

It was fitting that Congress opened its hearings on our new foreign military and economic aid programs in Washington at the very time that Mr. Khrushchev's words in Vienna were demonstrating as nothing else could the need for that very program. It should be well run and effectively administered, but I believe we must do it, and I hope that you, the American people, will support it again because I think it is vitally important to the security of these areas. There is no use talking against the Communist advance unless we are willing to meet our responsibilities, however burdensome they may be. . . .

Ten days later, the President again spoke of the need for action on this front.

Remarks at the National Conference on International Economic and Social Development, June 16, 1961

. . . In 1952 the free world was apprehensive of more Korea-type wars of invasion; today the primary threat to freedom arises internally from what the Communists cynically call "wars of liberation." . . .

. . . I have found in Washington and about the country a great desire "to do something": to bolster the defense of freedom, to stop the spread of Communism, to exercise initiative in world affairs. I have heard talk about new military commitments and new troop deployments. Extra funds have been voted for air power, and there is talk of additional antiguerrilla units. All of this is important. But Mr. Khrushchev's "wars of liberation" will not be stopped by B-58's. They cannot be deterred by military guarantees. And they cannot, for the most part, be resisted by American intervention in the absence of outside Communist intervention.

I therefore urge those who want to "do something" to channel their energies behind our new foreign aid program, to help prevent the social injustice and economic chaos which invite subversion and revolt, to encourage the social and economic reform and development that can stabilize new nations and weak governments, to train and equip the local forces upon whom must rest the chief burden of resisting local, Communist-supplied guerrillas.

Those who oppose foreign economic and military assistance should know that the Communists do not, that their aid to less-developed countries is sharply rising, that they have already sent some eight thousand technicians into these areas, and that they make credits available on a long-term basis, without subjecting the recipient country to the perils of an annual legislative renewal. Even in our own hemisphere, Communist bloc aid is dangled before the eyes of those who have long been devoted to freedom, but who long for an end to their poverty.

In short, there is no point in speaking out against the spread of Communism if we are unwilling to recognize which weapons are most needed in that struggle. There is no point in calling for vigorous action to protect our security if we are unwilling to pay the price and carry the burdens which are necessary to maintain that security. And, as the late Arthur Vandenberg said a long time ago, there is no point in responding to the shouts of a man drowning twenty feet from shore by throwing him a ten-foot rope. . . .

PEACE CORPS

Surely the most distinctive innovation of the new Administration was the Peace Corps. It had—and has—two of the most appealing characteristics of the new Administration— youth and dedication. It also faced the gravest of problems. In a special message to the Congress the President outlined in full detail the plans for the new venture.

Special Message to the Congress on the Peace Corps, March 1, 1961

I recommend to the Congress the establishment of a permanent Peace Corps, *a pool of trained American men and women sent overseas by the U.S. Government or through private organizations and institutions to help foreign countries meet their urgent needs for skilled manpower.* . . .

Throughout the world the people of the newly developing

nations are struggling for economic and social progress which reflects their deepest desires. Our own freedom, and the future of freedom around the world, depend . . . on their ability to build growing and independent nations where men can live in dignity, liberated from the bonds of hunger, ignorance and poverty.

One of the greatest obstacles to the achievement of this goal is the lack of trained men and women with the skill to teach the young and assist in the operation of development projects, men and women with the capacity to cope with the demands of swiftly evolving economies, and with the dedication to put that capacity to work in the villages, the mountains, the towns and the factories of dozens of struggling nations.

The vast task of economic development urgently requires skilled people to do the work of the society: to help teach in the schools, construct development projects, demonstrate modern methods of sanitation in the villages, and perform a hundred other tasks calling for training and advanced knowledge.

To meet this urgent need for skilled manpower we are proposing the establishment of a Peace Corps, an organization which will recruit and train American volunteers, sending them abroad to work with the people of other nations.

This organization will differ from existing assistance programs in that its members will supplement technical advisers by offering the specific skills needed by developing nations if they are to put technical advice to work. They will help provide the skilled manpower necessary to carry out the development projects planned by the host governments, acting at a working level and serving at great personal sacrifice. There is little doubt that the number of those who wish to serve will be far greater than our capacity to absorb them. . . .

Most heartening of all, the initial reaction to this proposal has been an enthusiastic response by student groups, professional organizations and private citizens everywhere, a convincing demonstration that we have in this country an immense reservoir of dedicated men and women willing to devote their energies and time and toil to the cause of world peace and human progress.

Among the specific programs to which Peace Corps members can contribute are: teaching in primary and secondary schools, especially as part of national English-language-teaching programs; participation in the world-wide program of malaria eradication; instruction and operation of public health and sanitation projects; aiding in village development through school construction and other programs; increasing rural agricultural productivity by assisting local farmers to use modern implements and techniques. The initial emphasis of these programs will be on teaching. . . .

The Peace Corps will not be limited to the young, or to college graduates. All Americans who are qualified will be welcome to join this effort. But undoubtedly the Corps will be made up primarily of young people as they complete their formal education.

Because one of the greatest resources of a free society is the strength and diversity of its private organizations and institutions, much of the Peace Corps program will be carried out by these groups, financially assisted by the Federal Government.

Peace Corps personnel will be made available to developing nations in the following ways:

1. Through private voluntary agencies carrying on international assistance programs.

2. Through overseas programs of colleges and universities.

3. Through assistance programs of international agencies.

4. Through assistance programs of the United States Government.

5. Through new programs which the Peace Corps itself directly administers. . . .

In all instances the men and women of the Peace Corps will go only to those countries where their services and skills are genuinely needed and desired. . . .

Length of service in the Corps will vary depending on the kind of project and the country, generally ranging from two to three years. Peace Corps members will often serve under conditions of physical hardship, living under primitive conditions among the people of developing nations. For every Peace Corps member service will mean a great financial sacrifice. They will receive no salary. Instead they will be given an allowance which will only be sufficient to meet their basic needs and maintain health. It is essential that Peace Corpsmen and women live simply and unostentatiously among the people they have come to assist. At the conclusion of their tours, members of the Peace Corps will receive a small sum in the form of severance pay based on length of service abroad, to assist them during their first weeks back in the United States. Service with the Peace Corps will not exempt volunteers from Selective Service. . . .

Although this is an American Peace Corps, the problem of world development is not just an American problem. Let us hope that other nations will mobilize the spirit and energies and skill of their people in some form of Peace Corps, making our own effort only one step in a major international effort to increase the welfare of all men and improve understanding among nations.

Selection and training of the volunteers proceeded as planned. In the meantime, the Congress considered legislation to put the Corps on a permanent basis. By September, when the bill was passed and funds were appropriated, the first groups of trainees were on their way to teach in Ghana and to survey the back country of Tanganyika.

The bill providing a $3.9 billion appropriation was one of the last pieces of legislation to come out of Congress before it adjourned. The Congress had previously approved most of the foreign-aid program, including the new Agency for International Development, but did not approve the formula for long-term financing proposed by the President.

CHAPTER XI
ALLIANCE FOR PROGRESS

"TO OUR SISTER REPUBLICS SOUTH OF OUR BORDER, WE OFFER A SPECIAL PLEDGE: TO CONVERT OUR GOOD WORDS INTO GOOD DEEDS, IN A NEW ALLIANCE FOR PROGRESS. . . ."

"LET US ONCE AGAIN AWAKEN OUR AMERICAN REVOLUTION UNTIL IT GUIDES THE STRUGGLES OF PEOPLE EVERYWHERE—NOT WITH AN IMPERIALISM OF FORCE OR FEAR—BUT THROUGH THE RULE OF COURAGE AND FREEDOM AND HOPE FOR THE FUTURE OF MAN."

". . . I HAVE CALLED ON ALL THE PEOPLE OF THE HEMISPHERE TO JOIN IN A NEW ALLIANCE FOR PROGRESS—*Alianza para Progreso*—. . . TO SATISFY THE BASIC NEEDS OF THE AMERICAN PEOPLE FOR HOMES, WORK AND LAND, HEALTH AND SCHOOLS—*techo, trabajo y tierra, salud y escuela.*"

When World War II ended, the relations of the United States with Latin America began a long, slow deterioration, unnoticed at first, but by the late 1950's shockingly evident. To Americans comfortably wrapped in memories of the Good Neighbor era, the stoning of Mr. Nixon in Venezuela in May, 1958, was a "fire bell in the night." Mr. Castro completed the rude awakening.

Early in his Administration, President Kennedy exhibited a keen interest in inter-American affairs, and expressed that interest in memorable terms. Perhaps the clearest reflection of his views is to be found in an address which he gave on March 13. Here are selections from that address:

INTER-AMERICAN RELATIONS

Address at a Reception for Latin-American Diplomats,
March 13, 1961

. . . For the first time we have the capacity to strike off the remaining bonds of poverty and ignorance, to free our people for the spiritual and intellectual fulfillment which has always been the goal of our civilization.

Yet at this very moment of maximum opportunity, we confront the same forces which have imperiled America throughout its history, the alien forces which once again seek to impose the despotisms of the old world on the people of the new. . . .

Our . . . task is to demonstrate to the entire world that man's unsatisfied aspiration for economic progress and social justice can best be achieved by free men working within a framework of democratic institutions. If we can do this in our own hemisphere, and for our own people, we may yet realize the prophecy of the great Mexican patriot, Benito Juárez, that "democracy is the destiny of future humanity." . . .

Therefore I have called on all the people of the hemisphere to join in a new Alliance for Progress—*Alianza para Progreso*—a vast co-operative effort, unparalleled in magnitude and nobility of purpose, to satisfy the basic needs of the American people for homes, work and land, health and schools —*techo, trabajo y tierra, salud y escuela.*

First, I propose that the American Republics begin on a vast new Ten-Year Plan for the Americas, a plan to transform the 1960's into an historic decade of democratic progress.

These ten years will be the years of maximum progress, maximum effort, the years when the greatest obstacles must be overcome, the years when the need for assistance will be the greatest. . . .

Let me stress that only the most determined efforts of the American nations themselves can bring success to this effort. They, and they alone, can mobilize their resources, enlist the energies of their people, and modify their social patterns so that all, and not just a privileged few, share in the fruits of growth. If this effort is made, then outside assistance will give a vital impetus to progress; without it, no amount of help will advance the welfare of the people.

Thus, if the countries of Latin America are ready to do their part, and I am sure they are, then I believe the United States, for its part, should help provide resources of a scope and magnitude sufficient to make this bold development plan a success, just as we helped to provide, against equal odds nearly, the resources adequate to help rebuild the economies of Western Europe. For only an effort of towering dimensions can insure fulfillment of our plan for a decade of progress.

Second, I will shortly request a ministerial meeting of the Inter-American Economic and Social Council, a meeting at which we can begin the massive planning effort which will be at the heart of the Alliance for Progress.

For if our Alliance is to succeed, each Latin nation must formulate long-range plans for its own development, plans which establish targets and priorities, insure monetary stability, establish the machinery for vital social change, stimulate private activity and initiative, and provide for a maximum national effort. These plans will be the foundation of our development effort, and the basis for the allocation of outside resources. . . .

Third, I have this evening signed a request to the Congress for $500 million as a first step in fulfilling the Act of Bogotá. This is the first large-scale inter-American effort, instituted by my predecessor President Eisenhower, to attack the social barriers which block economic progress. The money will be used to combat illiteracy, improve the productivity and use of the land, wipe out disease, attack archaic tax and land tenure structures, provide educational opportunities and offer a broad range of projects designed to make the benefits of increasing abundance available to all. . . .

Fourth, we must support all economic integration which is a genuine step toward larger markets and greater competitive opportunity. The fragmentation of Latin-American economies is a serious barrier to industrial growth. Projects such as the Central American common market and free trade areas in South America can help to remove these obstacles.

Fifth, the United States is ready to co-operate in serious, case-by-case examinations of commodity market problems. Frequent violent changes in commodity prices seriously injure the economies of many Latin-American countries, draining their resources, and stultifying their growth. . . .

Sixth, we will immediately step up our Food-for-Peace emergency program, help to establish food reserves in areas of recurrent drought, and help provide school lunches for children and offer feed grains for use in rural development. . . .

Seventh, all the people of the hemisphere must be allowed to share in the expanding wonders of science, wonders which have captured man's imagination, challenged the powers of his mind, and given him the tools for rapid progress. I invite Latin-American scientists to work with us in new projects in fields such as medicine and agriculture, physics and astronomy and desalinization; and to help plan for regional research laboratories in these and other fields; and to strengthen co-operation between American universities and laboratories.

We also intend to expand our science-teacher-training programs to include Latin-American instructors, to assist in establishing such programs in other American countries, and translate and make available revolutionary new teaching materials in physics, chemistry, biology and mathematics, so that the young of all nations may contribute their skills to the advance of science.

Eighth, we must rapidly expand the training of those needed to man the economies of rapidly developing countries. This means expanded technical training programs, for which the Peace Corps, for example, will be available when needed. It also means assistance to Latin-American universities, graduate schools and research institutes.

We welcome proposals in Central America for intimate co-operation in higher education, co-operation which can achieve a regional effort of increased effectiveness and excellence. We are ready to help fill the gap in trained manpower, realizing that our ultimate goal must be a basic education for all who wish to learn.

Ninth, we reaffirm our pledge to come to the defense of any American nation whose independence is endangered. As its confidence in the collective security system of the Organization of American States spreads, it will be possible to devote to constructive use a major share of those resources now spent on the instruments of war. Even now, as the government of Chile has said, the time has come to take the first steps toward sensible limitations of arms. And the new generation of military leaders has shown an increasing awareness that armies cannot only defend their countries; they can, as we have learned through our own Corps of Engineers, help to build them.

Tenth, we invite our friends in Latin America to contribute to the enrichment of life and culture in the United States. We need teachers of your literature and history and tradition, opportunities for our young people to study in your universities, access to your music, your art and the thought of your great philosophers. For we know we have much to learn. . . .

With steps such as these, we propose to complete the revolution of the Americas, to build a hemisphere where all men can hope for a suitable standard of living, and all can live out their lives in dignity and in freedom.

To achieve this goal political freedom must accompany material progress. Our Alliance for Progress is an alliance of free governments, and it must work to eliminate tyranny from a hemisphere in which it has no rightful place. Therefore let us express our special friendship to the people of Cuba and the Dominican Republic, and the hope they will soon rejoin the society of free men, uniting with us in our common effort.

This political freedom must be accompanied by social change. For unless necessary social reforms, including land and tax reform, are freely made; unless we broaden the opportunity of all of our people; unless the great mass of Americans share in increasing prosperity, then our alliance, our revolution, our dream and our freedom will fail. But we call for social change by free men, change in the spirit of Washington and Jefferson, of Bolívar and San Martín and Martí, not change which seeks to impose on men tyrannies which we cast out a century and a half ago. Our motto is what it has always been: "Progress yes, tyranny no—*Progreso sí, tiranía no!*"

But our greatest challenge comes from within, the task of creating an American civilization where spiritual and cultural values are strengthened by an ever-broadening base of material advance, where, within the rich diversity of its own traditions, each nation is free to follow its own path toward progress.

The completion of our task will, of course, require the efforts of all the governments of our hemisphere. But the efforts of governments alone will never be enough. In the end, the people must choose and the people must help themselves.

And so I say to the men and women of the Americas—to the *campesino* in the fields, to the *obrero* in the cities, to the *estudiante* in the schools: prepare your mind and heart for the task ahead, call forth your strength and let each devote his energies to the betterment of all, so that your children and our children in this hemisphere can find an ever richer and a freer life. . . .

ACT OF BOGOTA

In 1960, Congress had authorized $500 million for the Inter-American Fund for Social Progress, and on the basis of this action, the United States had subscribed to the Act of Bogotá, along with eighteen other American republics. In March, 1961, President Kennedy sent a message to Congress asking that this sum be appropriated, together with another $100 million that had been authorized for Chilean reconstruction. Both sums were appropriated in May. In the portions of this message quoted below, he set forth with great clarity the guiding lines of his Administration's policy toward Latin America.

Message to the Congress on Appropriation for the Act of Bogotá, March 14, 1961

The Act of Bogotá marks an historic turning point in the evolution of the Western Hemisphere. For the first time the American nations have agreed to join in a massive co-operative effort to strengthen democratic institutions through a program of economic development and social progress. . . .

The people of Latin America are the inheritors of a deep belief in political democracy and the freedom of man, a sincere faith that the best road to progress is freedom's road. But if the Act of Bogotá becomes just another empty declaration, if we are unwilling to commit our resources and energy to the task of social progress and economic development, then we face a grave and imminent danger that desperate peoples will turn to Communism or other forms of tyranny as their only hope for change. Well-organized, skillful and strongly financed forces are constantly urging them to take this course.

A few statistics will illustrate the depth of the problems of Latin America. This is the fastest-growing area in the world. Its current population of 195 million represents an increase of about 30 per cent over the past ten years, and by the 1980's the continent will have to support more than 400 million people. At the same time the average per capita annual product is only $280, less than one-ninth that of the United States; and in large areas, inhabited by millions of people, it is less than $70. Thus it is a difficult task merely to keep living standards from falling further as population grows.

Such poverty inevitably takes its toll in human life. The average American can expect to live seventy years, but life expectancy in Latin America is only forty-six, dropping to about thirty-five in some Central American countries. And while our rate of infant mortality is less than 30 per thousand, it is more than 110 per thousand in Latin America.

Perhaps the greatest stimulus to our own development was the establishment of universal basic education. But for most of the children of Latin America education is a remote and unattainable dream. Illiteracy extends to almost half the adults, reaching 90 per cent in one country. And approximately 50 per cent of school-age children have no schools to attend.

In one major Latin-American capital a third of the total population is living in filthy and unbearable slums. In another country 80 per cent of the entire population is housed in makeshift shacks and barracks, lacking the privacy of separate rooms for families.

It was to meet these shocking and urgent conditions that the

Act of Bogotá was signed. This Act, building on the concept of Operation Pan America initiated by Brazil in 1958, introduced two important new elements to the effort to improve living standards in South America.

First, the nations of Latin America have recognized the need for an intensive program of self-help: mobilizing their domestic resources, and undertaking basic reforms in tax structure, in land ownership and use, and in education, health and housing.

Second, it launches a major inter-American program for the social progress which is an indispensable condition to growth, a program for improved land use, education, health and housing. . . .

The $500 million Inter-American Fund for Social Progress is only the first move toward carrying out the declarations of the Act of Bogotá; and the Act itself is only a single step in our program for the development of the hemisphere, a program I have termed the Alliance for Progress. . . . In addition to the social fund, hemispheric development will require substantial outside resources for economic development, a major self-help effort by the Latin-American nations themselves, inter-American co-operation to deal with the problems of economic integration and commodity markets and other measures designed to speed economic growth and improve understanding among the American nations.

SOCIAL PROGRESS AND ECONOMIC DEVELOPMENT

The fund which I am requesting today will be devoted to social progress. Social progress is not a substitute for economic development. It is an effort to create a social framework within which all the people of a nation can share in the benefits of prosperity, and participate in the process of growth. Economic growth without social progress lets the great majority of the people remain in poverty, while a privileged few reap the benefits of rising abundance. In addition, the process of growth largely depends on the existence of beneficial social conditions. Our own experience is witness to this. For much of our own great productivity and industrial development is based on our system of universal public education.

Thus the purpose of our special effort for social progress is to overcome the barriers of geographical and social isolation, illiteracy and lack of educational opportunities, archaic tax and land tenure structures, and other institutional obstacles to broad participation in economic growth.

SELF-HELP AND INTERNAL REFORM

It is clear that the Bogotá program cannot have any significant impact if its funds are used merely for the temporary relief of conditions of distress. Its effectiveness depends on the willingness of each recipient nation to improve its own institutions, make necessary modifications in its own social patterns, and mobilize its own domestic resources for a program of development.

Even at the start such measures will be a condition of assistance from the social fund. Priorities will depend not merely on need, but on the demonstrated readiness of each government to make the institutional improvements which promise lasting social progress. The criteria for administration of the funds by the Inter-American Development Bank and the ICA will explicitly reflect these principles.

For example: the uneven distribution of land is one of the gravest social problems in many Latin-American countries. In some nations 2 per cent of the farms account for three-quarters of the total farm area. And in one Central American country, 40 per cent of the privately owned acreage is held in one-fifth of one per cent of the number of farms. It is clear that when land ownership is so heavily concentrated, efforts to increase agricultural productivity will only benefit a very small percentage of the population. Thus if funds for improving land usage are to be used effectively they should go to those nations in which the benefits will accrue to the great mass of rural workers.

EXAMPLES OF POTENTIAL AREAS OF PROGRESS

When each nation demonstrates its willingness to abide by these general principles, then outside resources will be focused on projects which have the greatest multiplying effect in mobilizing domestic resources, contributing to institutional reform, and in reducing the major obstacles to a development in which all can share.

In housing, for example, much can be done for middle-income groups through improved credit mechanisms. But, since the great majority of family incomes are only ten to fifty dollars a month, until income levels as a whole are increased, the most promising means of improving mass housing is through aided self-help projects, projects in which the low-income worker is provided with low-cost materials, land and some technical guidance, and then builds the house with his own labor, repaying the costs of materials with a long-term mortgage.

Education is another field where self-help efforts can effectively broaden educational opportunities, and a variety of techniques, from self-help school construction where the entire village contributes labor to the use of local people as part-time teachers, can be used.

In the field of land use there is no sharp demarcation between economic and social development. Improved land use and rural living conditions were rightly given top place in the Act of Bogotá. Most of the Latin-American peoples live and work on the land. Yet agricultural output and productivity have lagged far behind both industrial development and urgent needs for consumption and export.

As a result poverty, illiteracy, hopelessness and a sense of injustice, the conditions which breed political and social unrest, are almost universal in the Latin-American countryside.

Thus, there is an immediate need for higher and more diversified agricultural production, better distribution of wealth and income, and wider sharing in the process of development. This can be partly accomplished through establishing supervised rural credit facilities, helping to finance resettlement in new lands, constructing access roads to new settlement sites, conducting agricultural surveys and research, and introducing agricultural extension services.

CHAPTER XII
THE DEEPENING CRISIS

"A CITY DOES NOT BECOME FREE MERELY BY CALLING IT A 'FREE CITY.' FOR A CITY OR A PEOPLE TO BE FREE REQUIRES THAT THEY BE GIVEN THE OPPORTUNITY, WITHOUT ECONOMIC, POLITICAL OR POLICE PRESSURE, TO MAKE THEIR OWN CHOICE AND TO LIVE THEIR OWN LIVES."

"ANY DANGEROUS SPOT IS TENABLE IF MEN—BRAVE MEN—WILL MAKE IT SO."

"WE CANNOT NEGOTIATE WITH THOSE WHO SAY, 'WHAT'S MINE IS MINE AND WHAT'S YOURS IS NEGOTIABLE.' "

"[THEY] HAVE OFFERED TO TRADE US AN APPLE FOR AN ORCHARD. WE DON'T DO THAT IN THIS COUNTRY."

"PEACE AND FREEDOM DO NOT COME CHEAP, AND WE ARE DESTINED—ALL OF US HERE TODAY—TO LIVE OUT MOST IF NOT ALL OF OUR LIVES IN UNCERTAINTY AND CHALLENGE AND PERIL."

At the end of May the President made a trip to Europe. He spent some time in Paris with General de Gaulle, went on to Vienna for talks with Mr. Khrushchev, and returned by way of London. On his return he reported to the nation by television.

MEETINGS WITH DE GAULLE
AND KHRUSHCHEV

Report to the Nation,
June 6, 1961

... I returned this morning from a week-long trip to Europe and I want to report to you on that trip in full. It was in every sense an unforgettable experience. The people of Paris, of Vienna, of London, were generous in their greeting. They were heart-warming in their hospitality, and their graciousness to my wife is particularly appreciated.

We knew of course that the crowds and the shouts were meant in large measure for the country that we represented, which is regarded as the chief defender of freedom. Equally memorable was the pageantry of European history and culture that is very much a part of any ceremonial reception, to lay a wreath at the Arc de Triomphe, to dine at Versailles, at Schönbrunn Palace and with the Queen of England. These are the colorful memories that will remain with us for many years to come. Each of the three cities that we visited—Paris, Vienna and London—has existed for many centuries, and each serves as a reminder that the Western civilization that we seek to preserve has flowered over many years, and has defended itself over many centuries. But this was not a ceremonial trip. Two aims of American foreign policy, above all others, were the reason for the trip: the unity of the free world, whose strength is the security of us all, and the eventual achievement of a lasting peace. My trip was devoted to the advancement of these two aims.

To strengthen the unity of the West, our journey opened in

Paris and closed in London. My talks with General de Gaulle were profoundly encouraging to me. Certain differences in our attitudes on one or another problem became insignificant in view of our common commitment to defend freedom. Our alliance, I believe, became more secure, the friendship of our nation with theirs, I hope, became firmer, and the relations between the two of us who bear responsibility became closer, and I hope were marked by confidence. I found General de Gaulle far more interested in our frankly stating our position, whether or not it was his own, than in appearing to agree with him when we do not. But he knows full well the true meaning of an alliance. He is after all the only major leader of World War II who still occupies a position of great responsibility. His life has been one of unusual dedication; he is a man of extraordinary personal character, symbolizing the new strength and the historic grandeur of France. Throughout our discussions he took the long view of France and the world at large. I found him a wise counselor for the future, and an informative guide to the history that he has helped to make. Thus we had a valuable meeting.

I believe that certain doubts and suspicions that might have come up . . . were removed on both sides. Problems which proved to be not of substance but of wording or procedure were cleared away. No question, however sensitive, was avoided. No area of interest was ignored, and the conclusions that we reached will be important for the future—in our agreement on defending Berlin, on working to improve the defenses of Europe, on aiding the economic and political independence of the underdeveloped world, including Latin America, on spurring European economic unity, on concluding successfully the conference on Laos, and on closer consultations and solidarity in the Western alliance. . . .

The people of Vienna know what it is to live under occupation, and they know what it is to live in freedom. Their welcome to me as President of this country should be heart-warming to us all. I went to Vienna to meet the leader of the Soviet Union, Mr. Khrushchev. For two days we met in sober, intensive conversation, and I believe it is my obligation to the people, to the Congress and to our allies to report on those conversations candidly and publicly.

Mr. Khrushchev and I had a very full and frank exchange of views on the major issues that now divide our two countries. I will tell you now that it was a very sober two days. There was no discourtesy, no loss of tempers, no threats or ultimatums by either side; no advantage or concession was either gained or given; no major decision was either planned or taken; no spectacular progress was either achieved or pretended.

This kind of informal exchange may not be as exciting as a full-fledged summit meeting with a fixed agenda and a large corps of advisers, where negotiations are attempted and new agreements sought, but this was not intended to be and was not such a meeting, nor did we plan any future summit meetings at Vienna.

But I found this meeting with Chairman Khrushchev, as somber as it was, to be immensely useful. I had read his speeches and his published policies. I had been advised on his views. I had been told by other leaders of the West, General de Gaulle, Chancellor Adenauer, Prime Minister Macmillan, what manner of man he was.

But I bear the responsibility of the Presidency of the United

States, and it is my duty to make decisions that no adviser and no ally can make for me. It is my obligation and responsibility to see that these decisions are as informed as possible, that they are based on as much direct, firsthand knowledge as possible.

I therefore thought it was of immense importance that I know Mr. Khrushchev, that I gain as much insight and understanding as I could on his present and future policies. At the same time, I wanted to make certain Mr. Khrushchev knew this country and its policies, that he understood our strength and our determination, and that he knew that we desired peace with all nations of every kind.

I wanted to present our views to him directly, precisely, realistically, and with an opportunity for discussion and clarification. This was done. No new aims were stated in private that have not been stated in public on either side. The gap between us was not, in such a short period, materially reduced, but at least the channels of communication were opened more fully, at least the chances of a dangerous misjudgment on either side should now be less, and at least the men on whose decisions the peace in part depends have agreed to remain in contact.

This is important, for neither of us tried merely to please the other, to agree merely to be agreeable, to say what the other wanted to hear, and just as our judicial system relies on witnesses appearing in court and on cross-examination instead of hearsay testimony or affidavits on paper, so, too, was this direct give-and-take of immeasurable value in making clear and precise what we considered to be vital, for the facts of the matter are that the Soviets and ourselves give wholly different meanings to the same words—war, peace, democracy and popular will.

We have wholly different views of right and wrong, of what

is an internal affair and what is aggression, and, above all, we have wholly different concepts of where the world is and where it is going.

Only by such a discussion was it possible for me to be sure that Mr. Khrushchev knew how differently we view the present and the future. Our views contrasted sharply but at least we knew better at the end where we both stood. Neither of us was there to dictate a settlement or convert the other to a cause or to concede our basic interests. But both of us were there, I think, because we realized that each nation has the power to inflict enormous damage upon the other, that such a war could and should be avoided if at all possible since it would settle no dispute and prove no doctrine, and that care should thus be taken to prevent our conflicting interests from so directly confronting each other that war necessarily ensued.

We believe in a system of national freedom and independence. He believes in an expanding and dynamic concept of world Communism, and the question was whether these two systems can ever hope to live in peace without permitting any loss of security or any denial of freedom of our friends. However difficult it may seem to answer this question in the affirmative as we approach so many harsh tests, I think we owe it to all mankind to make every possible effort.

That is why I considered the Vienna talks useful. The somber mood that they conveyed was not cause for elation or relaxation, nor was it cause for undue pessimism or fear. It simply demonstrated how much work we in the free world have to do and how long and hard a struggle must be our fate as Americans in this generation as the chief defenders of the cause of liberty.

The one area which afforded some immediate prospect of accord was Laos. Both sides recognized the need to reduce the dangers in that situation. Both sides endorsed the concept of a neutral and independent Laos, much in the manner of Burma or Cambodia.

Of critical importance to the current conference on Laos in Geneva, both sides recognized the importance of an effective cease-fire. It is urgent that this be translated into new attitudes at Geneva, enabling the international control commission to do its duty, to make certain that a cease-fire is enforced and maintained. I am hopeful that progress can be made on this matter in the coming days at Geneva, for that would greatly improve international atmospheres.

No such hope emerged, however, with respect to the other deadlocked Geneva conference, seeking a treaty to ban nuclear tests. Mr. Khrushchev made it clear that there could not be a neutral administrator, in his opinion, because no one was truly neutral, that a Soviet veto would have to apply to acts of enforcement, that inspection was only a subterfuge for espionage in the absence of total disarmament, and that the present test ban negotiations appeared futile. In short, our hopes for an end to nuclear tests, for an end to the spread of nuclear weapons, and for some slowing down of the arms race have been struck a serious blow. Nevertheless, the stakes are too important for us to abandon the draft treaty we have offered at Geneva.

But our most somber talks were on the subject of Germany and Berlin. I made it clear to Mr. Khrushchev that the security of Western Europe and therefore our own security are deeply involved in our presence and our access rights to West Berlin, that those rights are based on law and not on sufferance, and that we are determined to maintain those rights at any risk, and thus meet our obligation to the people of West Berlin, and their right to choose their own future.

Mr. Khrushchev, in turn, presented his views in detail, and his presentation will be the subject of further communications. But we are not seeking to change the present situation. A binding German peace treaty is a matter for all who were at war with Germany, and we and our allies cannot abandon our obligations to the people of West Berlin.

Generally, Mr. Khrushchev did not talk in terms of war. He believes the world will move his way without resort to force. He spoke of his nation's achievements in space. He stressed his intention to outdo us in industrial production, to out-trade us, to prove to the world the superiority of his system over ours. Most of all, he predicted the triumph of Communism in the new and less-developed countries. . . .

My stay in England was short but the visit gave me a chance to confer privately again with Prime Minister Macmillan, just as others of our party in Vienna were conferring yesterday with General de Gaulle and Chancellor Adenauer. We all agreed that there is work to be done in the West and from our conversations have come agreed steps to get on with that work. Our day in London, capped by a meeting with Queen Elizabeth and Prince Philip, was a strong reminder at the end of a long journey that the West remains united in its determination to hold its standards.

May I conclude by saying simply that I am glad to be home. We have on this trip admired splendid places and seen stirring sights, but we are glad to be home. No demonstration of support abroad could mean so much as the support which you, the American people, have so generously given to our country.

With that support I am not fearful of the future. We must be patient. We must be courageous. We must accept both risks and burdens, but with the will and the work freedom will prevail.

THE BERLIN CRISIS

There could be no doubt that for 1961 Mr. Khrushchev had chosen Berlin as the chief battleground for the Cold War. This is not to say that he relieved the pressure on other major trouble spots around the world. But he did make unmistakably clear his intention that Berlin should be the chief issue. And he was reckless in his threats of nuclear devastation if he wasn't allowed to have his way.

Neither President Kennedy nor the people of the United States took Mr. Khrushchev lightly. The President took steps to clarify our position, and to prepare militarily for the grave collision of interests which the Soviet leader predicted. Tension mounted steadily in the late spring and early summer. On June 4 the Soviet Union delivered an aide-mémoire outlining its position and its demands. After consultation with the British and French, the United States made a formal reply. On July 19 President Kennedy issued the following statement:

Statement on Germany and Berlin,
July 19, 1961

In consultation and full agreement with its British and French allies, and with the benefit of the views of the Federal Republic of Germany, and after consultation with the other member governments of the North Atlantic Treaty Organization, the United States on Monday delivered through its Embassy in Moscow its reply to the *aide-mémoire* on Germany and Berlin received from the Soviet Government on June 4. Our reply speaks for itself and advances what I believe to be an irrefutable legal, moral and political position. In this statement I should like to convey to the American people and the people of the world the basic issues which underlie the somewhat more formal language of diplomacy.

The Soviet *aide-mémoire* is a document which speaks of peace but threatens to disturb it. It speaks of ending the abnormal situation in Germany but insists on making permanent its abnormal division. It refers to the Four Power Alliance of World War II but seeks the unilateral abrogation of the rights of the other three powers. It calls for new international agreements while preparing to violate existing ones. It offers certain assurances while making it plain that its previous assurances are not to be relied upon. It professes concern for the rights of the citizens of West Berlin while seeking to expose them to the immediate or eventual domination of a regime which permits no self-determination. Three simple facts are clear:

1. Today there is peace in Berlin, in Germany and in Europe. If that peace is destroyed by the unilateral actions of the Soviet Union, its leaders will bear a heavy responsibility before world opinion and history.

2. Today the people of West Berlin are free. In that sense it is already a "free city"—free to determine its own leaders and free to enjoy the fundamental human rights reaffirmed in the United Nations Charter.

3. Today the continued presence in West Berlin of the United States, the United Kingdom and France is by clear legal right, arising from war, acknowledged in many agreements signed by the Soviet Union, and strongly supported by the overwhelming majority of the people of that city. Their freedom is dependent upon our exercise of these rights—an exercise which is thus a political and moral obligation as well as a legal right. Inasmuch as these rights, including the right of access to Berlin, are not held from the Soviet Government, they cannot be ended by any unilateral action of the Soviet Union. They cannot be affected by a so-called "peace treaty," covering only a part of Germany, with a regime of the Soviet Union's own creation— a regime which is not freely representative of all or any part of Germany, and does not enjoy the confidence of the seventeen million East Germans. The steady stream of German refugees from East to West is eloquent testimony to that fact.

The United States has been prepared since the close of the war, and is prepared today, to achieve, in agreement with its World War II allies, a freely negotiated peace treaty covering all of Germany and based on the freely expressed will of all of the German people. We have never suggested that, in violation of international law and earlier Four Power agreements, we might legally negotiate a settlement with only a part of Germany, or without the participation of the other principal World War II allies. We know of no sound reason why the Soviet Government should now believe that the rights of the Western Powers, derived from Nazi Germany's surrender, could be invalidated by such an action on the part of the Soviet Union.

The United States has consistently sought the goal of a just and comprehensive peace treaty for all of Germany since first suggesting in 1946 that a special commission be appointed for this purpose. We still recognize the desirability of change—but it should be a change in the direction of greater, not less, freedom of choice for the people of Germany and Berlin. The Western Peace Plan and the All-Berlin solution proposed by the Western Allies at Geneva in 1959 were constructive, practical offers to obtain this kind of fair settlement in Central Europe. Our objective is not to perpetuate our presence in either Germany or Berlin—our objective is the perpetuation of the peace and freedom of their citizens.

But the Soviet Union has blocked all progress toward the conclusion of a just treaty based on the self-determination of the German people, and has instead repeatedly heightened world tensions over this issue. The Soviet Blockade of Berlin in 1948, the Soviet note of November 27, 1958, and this most recent Soviet *aide-mémoire* of June 4, 1961, has greatly disturbed the tranquillity of this area.

The real intent of the June 4 *aide-mémoire* is that East Berlin, a part of a city under Four Power status, would be formally absorbed into the so-called German Democratic Republic while West Berlin, even though called a "free city," would lose the protection presently provided by the Western Powers and become subject to the will of a totalitarian regime. Its leader, Herr Ulbricht, has made clear his intention, once this so-called "peace treaty" is signed, to curb West Berlin's communications with the free world and to suffocate the freedom it now enjoys.

The area thus newly subjected to Soviet threats of heightened tension poses no danger whatsoever to the peace of the world or to the security of any nation. The world knows that there is no reason for a crisis over Berlin today—and that, if one develops, it will be caused by the Soviet Government's attempt to invade the rights of others and manufacture tensions. It is, moreover, misusing the words "freedom" and "peace." For, as our reply states, "freedom" and "peace" are not merely words —nor can they be achieved by words or promises alone. They are representative of a state of affairs.

A city does not become free merely by calling it a "free city." For a city or a people to be free requires that they be given the opportunity, without economic, political or police pressure, to make their own choice and to live their own lives. The people of West Berlin today have that freedom. It is the objective of our policy that they shall continue to have it.

Peace does not come automatically from a "peace treaty." There is peace in Germany today even though the situation is "abnormal." A "peace treaty" that adversely affects the lives and rights of millions will not bring peace with it. A "peace treaty" that attempts to affect adversely the solemn commitments of three great powers will not bring peace with it. We again urge the Soviet Government to reconsider its course, to return to the path of constructive co-operation it so frequently states it desires, and to work with its World War II allies in concluding a just and enduring settlement of issues remaining from that conflict.

Six days later the President addressed the nation on television.

Report to the Nation on the Berlin Crisis,
July 25, 1961

Seven weeks ago tonight I returned from Europe to report on my meeting with Premier Khrushchev and the others. His grim warnings about the future of the world, his *aide-mémoire* on Berlin, his subsequent speeches and threats which he and his agents have launched, and the increase in the Soviet military budget that he has announced, have all prompted a series of decisions by the Administration and a series of consultations with the members of the North Atlantic Treaty Organization. In Berlin, as you recall, he intends to bring to an end, through a stroke of the pen, first, our legal rights to be in West Berlin and, second, our ability to make good on our commitment to the two million free people of that city. That we cannot permit.

We are clear about what must be done, and we intend to do it. I want to talk frankly with you tonight about the first steps that we shall take. These actions will require sacrifice on the part of many of our citizens. More will be required in the future. They will require, from all of us, courage and perseverance in the years to come. But if we and our allies act out of strength and unity of purpose, with calm determination and steady nerves, using restraint in our words as well as our weapons, I am hopeful that both peace and freedom will be sustained.

The immediate threat to free men is in West Berlin. But that isolated outpost is not an isolated problem. The threat is world-wide. Our effort must be equally wide and strong, and not be obsessed by any single manufactured crisis. We face a challenge in Berlin, but there is also a challenge in Southeast Asia, where the borders are less guarded, the enemy harder to find, and the danger of Communism less apparent to those who have so little. We face a challenge in our own hemisphere, and indeed wherever else the freedom of human beings is at stake.

Let me remind you that the fortunes of war and diplomacy left the free people of West Berlin in 1945 110 miles behind the Iron Curtain. . . .

We are there as a result of our victory over Nazi Germany, and our basic rights to be there deriving from that victory include both our presence in West Berlin and the enjoyment of access across East Germany. These rights have been repeatedly confirmed and recognized in special agreements with the Soviet Union. Berlin is not a part of East Germany, but a separate territory under the control of the allied powers. Thus our rights there are clear and deep-rooted. But in addition to those rights is our commitment to sustain, and defend, if need be, the opportunity for more than two million people to determine their own future and choose their own way of life.

Thus, our presence in West Berlin, and our access thereto, cannot be ended by any act of the Soviet Government. The NATO shield was long ago extended to cover West Berlin, and we have given our word that an attack upon that city will be regarded as an attack upon us all.

For West Berlin, lying exposed 110 miles inside East Germany, surrounded by Soviet troops and close to Soviet supply lines, has many roles. It is more than a showcase of liberty, a symbol, an island of freedom in a Communist sea. It is even more than a link with the free world, a beacon of hope behind the Iron Curtain, an escape hatch for refugees.

West Berlin is all of that. But above all it has now become, as never before, the great testing place of Western courage and will, a focal point where our solemn commitments, stretching back over the years since 1945, and Soviet ambitions now meet in basic confrontation.

It would be a mistake for others to look upon Berlin, because of its location, as a tempting target. The United States is there; the United Kingdom and France are there; the pledge of NATO is there; and the people of Berlin are there. It is as secure, in that sense, as the rest of us, for we cannot separate its safety from our own.

I hear it said that West Berlin is militarily untenable. And so was Bastogne. And so, in fact, was Stalingrad. Any dangerous spot is tenable if men—brave men—will make it so.

We do not want to fight, but we have fought before. And others in earlier times have made the same dangerous mistake of assuming that the West was too selfish and too soft and too divided to resist invasions of freedom in other lands. Those who threaten to unleash the forces of war on a dispute over West Berlin should recall the words of the ancient philosopher: "A man who causes fear cannot be free from fear."

We cannot and will not permit the Communists to drive us out of Berlin, either gradually or by force. For the fulfillment of our pledge to that city is essential to the morale and security of Western Germany, to the unity of Western Europe, and to the faith of the entire free world. Soviet strategy has long been aimed, not merely at Berlin, but at dividing and neutralizing all of Europe, forcing us back to our own shores. We must meet our oft-stated pledge to the free peoples of West Berlin, and maintain our rights and their safety, even in the face of force, in order to maintain the confidence of other free peoples in our word and our resolve. The strength of the alliance on which our security depends is dependent in turn on our willingness to meet our commitments to them.

So long as the Communists insist that they are preparing to end by themselves unilaterally our rights in West Berlin and our commitments to its people, we must be prepared to defend those rights and those commitments. We will at all times be ready to talk, if talk will help. But we must also be ready to resist with force, if force is used upon us. Either alone would fail. Together, they can serve the cause of freedom and peace.

The new preparations that we shall make to defend the peace are part of the long-term build-up in our strength which has been under way since January. They are based on our needs to meet a world-wide threat, on a basis which stretches far beyond the present Berlin crisis. Our primary purpose is neither propaganda nor provocation, but preparation.

A first need is to hasten progress toward the military goals which the North Atlantic allies have set for themselves. In Europe today nothing less will suffice. We will put even greater resources into fulfilling those goals, and we look to our allies to do the same.

The supplementary defense build-ups that I asked from the Congress in March and May have already started moving us toward these and our other defense goals. They included an increase in the size of the Marine Corps, improved readiness of our reserves, expansion of our air- and sealift, and stepped-up procurement of needed weapons, ammunition and other items. To insure a continuing invulnerable capacity to deter or destroy any aggressor, they provided for the strengthening of our missile power and for putting 50 per cent of our B-52 and B-47 bombers on a ground alert which would send them on their way with fifteen minutes' warning.

These measures must be speeded up, and still others must now be taken. We must have sea- and airlift capable of moving our forces quickly and in large numbers to any part of the world.

But even more important, we need the capability of placing in any critical area at the appropriate time a force which, combined with those of our allies, is large enough to make clear our determination and our ability to defend our rights at all costs, and to meet all levels of aggressor pressure with whatever levels of force are required. We intend to have a wider choice than humiliation or all-out nuclear action.

While it is unwise at this time either to call up or send abroad excessive numbers of these troops before they are needed, let me make it clear that I intend to take, as time goes on, whatever steps are necessary to make certain that such forces can be deployed at the appropriate time without lessening our ability to meet our commitments elsewhere.

Thus, in the days and months ahead, I shall not hesitate to ask the Congress for additional measures, or exercise any of the executive powers that I possess to meet this threat to peace. Everything essential to the security of freedom must be done; and if that should require more men, or more taxes, or more controls, or other new powers, I shall not hesitate to ask for them. . . .

. . . I am well aware of the fact that many American families will bear the burden of these requests. Studies or careers will be interrupted; husbands and sons will be called away; incomes in some cases will be reduced. But these are burdens which must be borne if freedom is to be defended; Americans have willingly borne them before, and they will not flinch from the task now. . . .

. . . I must emphasize again that the choice is not merely between resistance and retreat, between atomic holocaust and surrender. Our peacetime military posture is traditionally defensive; but our diplomatic posture need not be. Our response to the Berlin crisis will not be merely military or negative. It will be more than merely standing firm. For we do not intend to leave it to others to choose and monopolize the forum and the framework of discussion. We do not intend to abandon our duty to mankind to seek a peaceful solution.

As signers of the United Nations Charter, we shall always be prepared to discuss international problems with any and all nations that are willing to talk, and listen, with reason. If they have proposals, not demands, we shall hear them. If they seek genuine understanding, not concessions of our rights, we shall meet with them. We have previously indicated our readiness to remove any actual irritants in West Berlin, but the freedom of that city is not negotiable. We cannot negotiate with those who say, "What's mine is mine and what's yours is negotiable." But we are willing to consider any arrangement or treaty in Germany consistent with the maintenance of peace and freedom, and with the legitimate security interests of all nations.

We recognize the Soviet Union's historical concerns about their security in Central and Eastern Europe, after a series of ravaging invasions, and we believe arrangements can be worked out which will help to meet those concerns, and make it possible for both security and freedom to exist in this troubled area.

For it is not the freedom of West Berlin which is "abnormal" in Germany today, but the situation in that entire divided country. If anyone doubts the legality of our rights in Berlin, we are ready to have it submitted to international adjudication. If anyone doubts the extent to which our presence is desired by the people of West Berlin, compared to East German feelings about their regime, we are ready to have that question submitted to a free vote in Berlin and, if possible, among all the German people. And let us hear at that time from the two and one-half million refugees who have fled the Communist regime in East Germany, voting for Western-type freedom with their feet.

The world is not deceived by the Communist attempt to label Berlin as a hotbed of war. There is peace in Berlin today. The source of world trouble and tension is Moscow, not Berlin. And if war begins, it will have begun in Moscow and not Berlin.

For the choice of peace or war is largely theirs, not ours. It is the Soviets who have stirred up this crisis. It is they who are trying to force a change. It is they who have opposed free elections. It is they who have rejected an all-German peace treaty, and the rulings of international law. And as Americans know from our history on our own old frontier, gun battles are caused by outlaws, and not by officers of the peace.

In short, while we are ready to defend our interests, we shall also be ready to search for peace, in quiet, exploratory talks, in formal or informal meetings. We do not want military considerations to dominate the thinking of either East or West. And Mr. Khrushchev may find that his invitation to other nations to join in a meaningless treaty may lead to *their* inviting *him* to join in the community of peaceful men, in abandoning the use of force, and in respecting the sanctity of agreements.

While all of these efforts go on, we must not be diverted from our total responsibilities, from other dangers, from other tasks. If new threats in Berlin or elsewhere should cause us to weaken our program of assistance to the developing nations who are also under heavy pressure from the same source, or to halt our efforts for realistic disarmament, or to disrupt or slow down our economy, or to neglect the education of our children, then those threats will surely be the most successful and least costly maneuver in Communist history. For we can afford all these efforts, and more, but we cannot afford *not* to meet this challenge.

And the challenge is not to us alone. It is a challenge to every nation which asserts its sovereignty under a system of liberty. It is a challenge to all who want a world of free choice. It is a special challenge to the Atlantic Community, the heartland of human freedom.

We in the West must move together in building military strength. We must consult one another more closely than ever before. We must together design our proposals for peace, and labor together as they are pressed at the conference table. And together we must share the burdens and the risks of this effort.

The Atlantic Community, as we know it, has been built in response to challenge: the challenge of European chaos in 1947; of the Berlin blockade in 1948, the challenge of Communist aggression in Korea in 1950. Now, standing strong and prosperous, after an unprecedented decade of progress, the Atlantic Community will not forget either its history or the principles which gave it meaning.

The solemn vow each of us gave to West Berlin in time of peace will not be broken in time of danger. If we do not meet our commitments to Berlin, where will we later stand? If we are not true to our word there, all that we have achieved in collective security, which relies on these words, will mean nothing. And if there is one path above all others to war, it is the path of weakness and disunity.

Today, the endangered frontier of freedom runs through divided Berlin. We want it to remain a frontier of peace. This is the hope of every citizen of the Atlantic Community; every citizen of Eastern Europe; and, I am confident, every citizen of the Soviet Union. For I cannot believe that the Russian people, who bravely suffered enormous losses in the Second World War, would now wish to see the peace upset once more in Germany. The Soviet Government alone can convert Berlin's frontier of peace into a pretext for war.

The steps I have indicated tonight are aimed at avoiding that war. To sum it all up: we seek peace, but we shall not surrender. That is the central meaning of this crisis, and the meaning of your government's policy.

With your help, and the help of other free men, this crisis can be surmounted. Freedom can prevail, and peace can endure.

I would like to close with a personal word. When I ran for the Presidency of the United States, I knew that this country faced serious challenges, but I could not realize, nor could any man realize who does not bear the burdens of this office, how heavy and constant would be those burdens.

Three times in my lifetime our country and Europe have been involved in major wars. In each case serious misjudgments were made on both sides of the intentions of others, which brought about great devastation.

Now, in the thermonuclear age, any misjudgment on either side about the intentions of the other could rain more devastation in several hours than has been wrought in all the wars of human history.

Therefore I, as President and Commander-in-Chief, and all of us as Americans, are moving through serious days. I shall bear this responsibility under our Constitution for the next three and one-half years, but I am sure that we all, regardless of our occupations, will do our very best for our country, and for our cause. For all of us want to see our children grow up in a country at peace, and in a world where freedom endures.

I know that sometimes we get impatient, we wish for some immediate action that would end our perils. But I must tell you that there is no quick and easy solution. The Communists control over a billion people, and they recognize that if we should falter, their success would be imminent.

We must look to long days ahead, which if we are courageous and persevering can bring us what we all desire.

In these days and weeks I ask for your help, and your advice. I ask for your suggestions, when you think we could do better.

All of us, I know, love our country, and we shall all do our best to serve it.

In meeting my responsibilities in these coming months as President, I need your good will, and your support and, above all, your prayers.

Thank you, and good night.

In other parts of his address the President said that he was asking Congress for an additional $3.247 billion of appropriations for the Armed Forces, about one half of it for the procurement of non-nuclear weapons, ammunition and equipment; requesting an increase in the Army's total authorized strength from 875,000 to about 1,000,000; requesting an increase of 29,000 and 63,000 men respectively in the active-duty strength of the Navy and Air Force; ordering that draft calls be doubled and tripled; asking Congress for authority to call up reserve units and individuals; ordering retention in active service or reactivation of ships and planes headed for retirement.

CHAPTER XIII
TO KEEP THE PEACE

"FOR DISARMAMENT WITHOUT CHECKS IS BUT A SHADOW, AND A COMMUNITY WITHOUT LAW IS BUT A SHELL."

"IT IS THEREFORE OUR INTENTION TO CHALLENGE THE SOVIET UNION, NOT TO AN ARMS RACE, BUT TO A PEACE RACE; TO ADVANCE WITH US STEP BY STEP, STAGE BY STAGE, UNTIL GENERAL AND COMPLETE DISARMAMENT HAS ACTUALLY BEEN ACHIEVED."

". . . THERE IS NO IGNORING THE FACT THAT THE TIDE OF SELF-DETERMINATION HAS NOT YET REACHED THE COMMUNIST EMPIRE. . . . LET US DEBATE COLONIALISM IN FULL, AND APPLY THE PRINCIPLE OF FREE CHOICE AND THE PRACTICE OF FREE PLEBISCITES IN EVERY CORNER OF THE GLOBE."

". . . HOWEVER CLOSE WE SOMETIMES SEEM TO THAT DARK AND FINAL ABYSS, LET NO MAN OF PEACE AND FREEDOM DESPAIR. . . . IF WE ALL CAN PERSEVERE, IF WE CAN IN EVERY LAND . . . LOOK BEYOND OUR OWN SHORES AND AMBITIONS, THEN SURELY THE AGE WILL DAWN IN WHICH THE STRONG ARE JUST AND THE WEAK SECURE AND THE PEACE PRESERVED."

"TOGETHER WE SHALL SAVE OUR PLANET OR TOGETHER WE SHALL PERISH IN ITS FLAMES."

Pushed off the front pages by the explosive events of a world in turmoil, the patient search for a disarmament formula continued throughout the year. Beginning with his Inaugural Address, the President alluded to the subject time and again in his major speeches. Indeed one of the distinctive marks of the Kennedy Administration has been its determination to leave no stone unturned in the search for a path to disarmament that would be compatible with national security and would deliver the world from the threat of nuclear holocaust.

In his second State of the Union Message, the President spoke of a test-ban treaty as "the first significant but essential step on the road to disarmament." Despite the earnest efforts of the United States, that first step was not taken.

The background is well reflected in two press conference statements by the President, one in May and the other in August.

NUCLEAR TESTING

This week Ambassador Arthur H. Dean has reported to me upon the status of the nuclear test ban conference at Geneva. On the opening day of the resumed conference, the United States, in closest co-operation with the United Kingdom, presented a series of new proposals; and on April 18, 1961, presented a complete nuclear test ban draft treaty. The new U.S. position represents an earnest and reasonable effort to reach a workable agreement. It constitutes a most significant over-all move in these negotiations. Unfortunately, the Soviet Union has introduced a new proposition into the negotiations which amounts to a built-in veto of an inspection system.

The Soviet proposal calls for a three-man administrative council to direct inspection operations and other activities of the control arrangements. This proposal reverses a position to which the Soviet Union has previously agreed. In earlier negotiations before this session in Geneva, it had been agreed that the inspection system would be headed by a single administrator, operating within a mandate clearly defined in the treaty. The Soviet Union would substitute a directorate, representing the Communist bloc, the Western nations and uncommitted countries. Each member of this triumvirate would have to agree with every other member before any action could be taken; even relatively detailed elements of the inspection system would be subject to a veto or a debating delay.

We recognize that the Soviet Union put forward its proposition before it had considered our new proposals. It is now considering our draft treaty, and we hope it will do so in a positive manner, as of course we are most anxious to secure an agreement in this vital area, a responsible and effective agreement. . . .

Fifteenth Press Conference,
August 10, 1961

. . . I am asking Ambassador Dean to return to Geneva on August 24, in an effort to ascertain whether the Soviet Union is now preparing to bring a safeguarded test ban agreement into being.

It is my hope that he will succeed in convincing the Soviet representatives that the test ban treaty which we have proposed, and stand ready to use as a basis for serious negotiations, is a necessary and rational means of reducing the likelihood of nuclear war, and if we were successful, would be an admirable beginning on the long road toward general disarmament.

His return to Geneva is with our hopes and prayers, and I believe with the hopes and prayers of all mankind, who are most concerned about further developments of this deadly weapon. This meeting is most important, most critical, and I am hopeful that we will find a favorable response by those who will participate in this negotiation.

But later events revealed that while Soviet representatives in Geneva were solemnly discussing a test ban formula, the

USSR was moving ahead with preparations for a series of nuclear tests in the atmosphere.

At the end of August, the Soviet Union without warning resumed nuclear testing. Mr. Khrushchev announced the first test—after it had happened—with a bellicose speech; and in succeeding days and weeks there followed a rapid succession of Soviet nuclear explosions. Months of careful preparation must have preceded this tightly scheduled series of tests.

The response from Washington was immediate. On August 30 the White House issued the following statement:

Statement issued by the White House, August 30, 1961

The Soviet Government's decision to resume nuclear weapons testing will be met with deepest concern and resentment throughout the world. The Soviet Government's decision to resume nuclear weapons testing presents a hazard to every human being throughout the world by increasing the dangers of nuclear fallout. The Soviet Government's decision to resume nuclear weapons testing is in utter disregard of the desire of mankind for a decrease in the arms race. The Soviet Government's decision to resume nuclear weapons testing presents a threat to the entire world by increasing the dangers of a thermonuclear holocaust. The Soviet Government's decision to resume nuclear weapons testing indicates the complete hypocrisy of its professions about general and complete disarmament.

For three years world attention has centered on the negotiations in Geneva for a treaty to secure an end to nuclear testing. Until last March it appeared that slow but encouraging progress had been made. At that time, the Soviet Union reversed its own earlier positions on key issues, refused to discuss seriously the genuine efforts made by the United States and the United Kingdom to meet known Soviet views, and blocked the path toward a nuclear test ban treaty. In order to avoid missing any possible opportunity to arrive at an agreement, the United States and the United Kingdom remained at the negotiating table. Only this week Ambassador Dean has made additional proposals in the hope of moving toward a test ban under effective international control. Urgent discussion of this issue had been scheduled at United States initiative at the forthcoming session of the General Assembly in the hopes that constructive debate could show the way to surmount the impasse at Geneva.

The pretext offered by the announcement for Soviet resumption of weapons testing is the very crisis which they themselves have created by threatening to disturb the peace which has existed in Germany and Berlin. It is not the first time they have made such charges against those who have dared to stand in the way of Soviet aggression. In addition, the announcement links the Soviet resumption of testing with threats of massive weapons which it must know cannot intimidate the rest of the world.

The purpose and motivation of this Soviet behavior now seems apparent: The Soviet Government wished to abandon serious negotiations in order to free its hand to resume nuclear weapons testing.

The United States continues to share the view of the people of the world as to the importance of an agreement to end nuclear weapons tests under effective safeguards. Such an agreement would represent a major breakthrough in the search for an end to the arms race. It would stop the accumulation of stockpiles of ever more powerful weapons. It would inhibit the spread of nuclear weapons to other countries with its increased risks of nuclear war.

These results, with their prospects for reducing the possibility of a nuclear war, have been blocked by the Soviet unilateral decision to resume nuclear testing. The Soviet Union bears a heavy responsibility before all humanity for this decision, a decision which was made in complete disregard of the United Nations. The termination of the moratorium on nuclear testing by the Soviet unilateral decision leaves the United States under the necessity of deciding what its own national interests require.

Under these circumstances, Ambassador Arthur Dean is being recalled immediately from Geneva.

Three days later President Kennedy and Prime Minister Macmillan of the United Kingdom made a statesmanlike offer:

Statement issued by the White House,
September 3, 1961

The President of the United States and the Prime Minister of the United Kingdom propose to Chairman Khrushchev that their three governments agree, effective immediately, not to conduct nuclear tests which take place in the atmosphere and produce radioactive fallout.

Their aim in this proposal is to protect mankind from the increasing hazards from atmospheric pollution and to contribute to the reduction of international tensions.

They urge Chairman Khrushchev to cable his immediate acceptance of this offer and his cessation of further atmospheric tests.

They further urge that their representatives at Geneva meet not later than September 9 to record this agreement and report it to the United Nations. They sincerely hope that the Soviet Union will accept this offer, which remains open for the period indicated.

They point out that with regard to atmospheric testing the United States and the United Kingdom are prepared to rely upon existing means of detection, which they believe to be adequate, and are not suggesting additional controls. But they affirm their serious desire to conclude a nuclear test ban treaty, applicable to other forms of testing as well, and regret that the Soviet Government has blocked such an agreement.

The offer was not accepted. On September 5, President Kennedy issued the following statement:

Statement from the White House,
September 5, 1961

In view of the continued testing by the Soviet Government, I have today ordered the resumption of nuclear tests, in the laboratory and underground, with no fallout. In our efforts to achieve an end to nuclear testing, we have taken every step that reasonable men could justify. In view of the acts of the Soviet Government, we must now take those steps which prudent men find essential. We have no other choice in fulfillment of the responsibilities of the United States Government to its own citizens and to the security of other free nations. Our offer to make an agreement to end all fallout tests remains open until September 9.

UNITED NATIONS ADDRESS

September was a month of tension and shock. Each day brought fresh news of Soviet nuclear testing in the atmosphere. Events in Berlin seemed to be moving nearer and nearer to a fateful climax. And then in mid-month Dag Hammarskjöld was killed in a plane accident in Africa—killed on a mission of peace.

The United Nations General Assembly opened in an atmosphere of anxiety and gloom. It was against this background that President Kennedy gave his memorable United Nations address on September 25.

Address to the United Nations,
September 25, 1961

I

We meet in an hour of grief and challenge. Dag Hammarskjöld is dead. But the United Nations lives on. His tragedy is deep in our hearts, but the task for which he died is at the top of our agenda. A noble servant of peace is gone. But the quest for peace lies before us.

The problem is not the death of one man; the problem is the life of this organization. It will either grow to meet the challenge of our age, or it will be gone with the wind, without influence, without force, without respect. Were we to let it die, to enfeeble its vigor, to cripple its powers, we would condemn the future.

For in the development of this organization rests the only true alternative to war, and war appeals no longer as a rational alternative. Unconditional war can no longer lead to unconditional victory. It can no longer serve to settle disputes. It can no longer be of concern to great powers alone. For a nuclear disaster, spread by winds and waters and fear, could well engulf the great and the small, the rich and the poor, the committed and the uncommitted alike. Mankind must put an end to war or war will put an end to mankind.

So let us here resolve that Dag Hammarskjöld did not live, or die, in vain. Let us call a truce to terror. Let us invoke the blessings of peace. And, as we build an international capacity to keep peace, let us join in dismantling the national capacity to wage war.

II

This will require new strength and new roles for the United Nations. For disarmament without checks is but a shadow, and a community without law is but a shell. Already the United Nations has become both the measure and the vehicle of man's most generous impulses. Already it has provided—in the Middle East, in Asia, in Africa this year in the Congo—a means to holding violence within bounds.

But the great question which confronted this body in 1945

is still before us: whether man's cherished hopes for progress and freedom are to be destroyed by terror and disruption; whether the "foul winds of war" can be tamed in time to free the cooling winds of reason; and whether the pledges of our Charter are to be fulfilled or defied: pledges to secure peace, progress, human rights and world law.

In this hall there are not three forces, but only two. One is composed of those who are trying to build the kind of world described in Articles I and II of the Charter. The other, seeking a far different world, would undermine this organization in the process.

Today of all days our dedication to that Charter must be maintained. It must be strengthened, first of all, by the selection of an outstanding civil servant to carry forward the responsibilities of the Secretary General, a man endowed with both the wisdom and the power to make meaningful the moral force of the world community. The late Secretary General nurtured and sharpened the United Nations' obligation to act. But he did not invent it. It was there in the Charter. It is still here in the Charter.

However difficult it may be to fill Mr. Hammarskjöld's place, it can better be filled by one man than by three. Even the three horses of the troika did not have three drivers, all going in different directions. They had only one, and so must the United Nations executive. To install a triumvirate, or any rotating authority, in the United Nations administrative offices would replace order with anarchy, action with paralysis, and confidence with confusion.

The Secretary General, in a very real sense, is the servant of the General Assembly. Diminish his authority and you diminish the authority of the only body where all nations, regardless of power, are equal and sovereign. Until all the powerful are just, the weak will be secure only in the strength of this Assembly.

Effective and independent executive action is not the same question as balanced representation. In view of the enormous change in the membership of this body since its founding, the American delegation will join in any effort for the prompt review and revision of the composition of United Nations bodies.

But to give this organization three drivers, to permit each great power in effect to decide its own case, would entrench the Cold War in the headquarters of peace. Whatever advantages such a plan may hold out to my country, as one of the great powers, we reject it. For we far prefer world law, in the age of self-determination, to world war, in the age of mass extermination.

III

Today, every inhabitant of this planet must contemplate the day when it may no longer be habitable. Every man, woman and child lives under a nuclear sword of Damocles, hanging by the slenderest of threads, capable of being cut at any moment by accident, miscalculation or madness. The weapons of war must be abolished before they abolish us.

Men no longer debate whether armaments are a symptom or cause of tension. The mere existence of modern weapons, ten million times more destructive than anything the world has ever seen, and only minutes away from any target on earth, is a source of horror and discord and distrust. Men no longer maintain that disarmament must await the settlement of all disputes, for disarmament must be a part of any permanent settlement. And men no longer pretend that the quest for disarmament is a sign of weakness, for in a spiraling arms race, a nation's security may well be shrinking even as its arms increase.

For fifteen years this organization has sought the reduction and destruction of arms. Now that goal is no longer a dream; it is a practical matter of life or death. The risks inherent in disarmament pale in comparison to the risks inherent in an unlimited arms race.

It is in this spirit that the recent Belgrade Conference, recognizing that this is no longer a Soviet problem or an American problem, but a human problem, endorsed a program of "general, complete and strictly an internationally controlled disarmament." It is in this same spirit that we in the United States have labored this year, with a new urgency, and with a new, now statutory agency fully endorsed by the Congress, to find an approach to disarmament which would be so far-reaching yet realistic, so mutually balanced and beneficial, that it could be accepted by every nation. And it is in this spirit that we have presented with the agreement of the Soviet Union, under the label both nations now accept of "general and complete disarmament," a new statement of newly agreed principles for negotiation.

But we are well aware that all issues of principle are not settled, and that principles alone are not enough. It is therefore our intention to challenge the Soviet Union, not to an arms race, but to a peace race: to advance with us step by step, stage by stage, until general and complete disarmament has actually been achieved. We invite them now to go beyond agreement in principle to reach agreement on actual plans.

The program to be presented to this Assembly, for general and complete disarmament under effective international control, moves to bridge the gap between those who insist on a gradual approach and those who talk only of the final and total achievement. It would create machinery to keep the peace as it destroys the machines of war. It would proceed through balanced and safeguarded stages designed to give no state a military advantage over another. It would place the final responsibility for verification and control where it belongs, not with the big powers alone, not with one's adversary or one's self, but in an international organization within the framework of the United Nations.

It would assure that indispensable condition of disarmament, true inspection, in stages proportionate to the stage of disarmament. It would cover delivery systems as well as weapons. It would ultimately halt their production as well as their testing, their transfer as well as their possession. It would achieve, under the eye of an international disarmament organization, a steady reduction in forces, both nuclear and conventional, until it had abolished all armies and all weapons except those needed for internal order and a new United Nations Peace Force. And it starts that process now, today, even as the talks begin.

In short, general and complete disarmament must no longer be a mere slogan, used to resist the first steps. It is no longer to be a goal without means of achieving it, without means of verifying its progress, without means of keeping the peace. It is now a realistic plan, and a test, a test of those only willing to talk and those willing to act.

Such a plan would not bring a world free from conflict or greed, but it would bring a world free from the terrors of mass destruction. It would not usher in the era of the super-state, but it would usher in an era in which no state could annihilate or be annihilated by another.

In 1945, this nation proposed the Baruch plan to internationalize the atom before other nations even possessed the bomb or demobilized their troops. We proposed with our allies the Disarmament Plan of 1951 while still at war in Korea. And we make our proposals today, while building up our defenses over Berlin, not because we are inconsistent or insincere or intimidated, but because we know the rights of free men will prevail, because while we are compelled against our will to rearm, we look confidently beyond Berlin to the kind of disarmed world we all prefer.

I therefore propose, on the basis of this plan, that disarmament negotiations resume promptly, and continue without interruption until an entire program for complete and general disarmament has not only been agreed upon but actually achieved.

IV

The logical place to begin is a treaty assuring the end of nuclear tests of all kinds, in every environment, under workable controls. The United States and the United Kingdom have proposed a treaty that is reasonable, effective and ready for signature. We are still prepared to sign that treaty today.

We also proposed a mutual ban on atmospheric testing, without inspection or controls, in order to save the human race from the poison of radioactive fallout. We regret that that offer was not accepted.

For fifteen years we have sought to make the atom an instrument of peaceful growth rather than war. But for fifteen years our concessions have been matched by obstruction, our patience by intransigence, and the pleas of mankind have been met with disregard.

Finally, as the explosions of others beclouded the skies my country was left no alternative but to act in the interests of its own and the free world's security. We cannot endanger that security by refraining from testing while others improve their arsenal. Nor can we endanger it by another long, un-inspected ban on testing. For three years we accepted those risks while seeking agreement on inspection. But this year, while we were negotiating in good faith at Geneva, others were secretly preparing new experiments in destruction.

Our tests are not polluting the atmosphere. Our deterrent weapons are guarded against accidental explosion or use. Our doctors and scientists stand ready to help any nation measure and meet the hazards to health which inevitably result from the tests in the atmosphere.

But to halt the spread of these terrible weapons, to halt the contamination of the air, to halt the spiraling nuclear arms race, we remain ready to seek new avenues of agreement. Our new disarmament program thus includes the following pro-posals:

First, signing the Test Ban Treaty, by all nations. This can be done now. Test ban negotiations need not and should not await general disarmament talks.

Second, stopping the production of fissionable materials for use in weapons, and preventing their transfer to any nation now lacking nuclear weapons.

Third, prohibiting the transfer of control over nuclear weapons to states that do not own them.

Fourth, keeping nuclear weapons from seeding new battle-grounds in outer space.

Fifth, gradually destroying existing nuclear weapons and converting their materials to peaceful uses.

Finally, halting the unlimited testing and production of strategic nuclear delivery vehicles, and gradually destroying them as well.

V

To destroy arms, however, is not enough. We must create even as we destroy, creating world-wide law and law enforce-ment as we outlaw world-wide war and weapons. In the world we seek, United Nations Emergency Forces which have been hastily assembled, uncertainly supplied and inadequately financed will never be enough.

Therefore, the United States recommends that all member nations earmark special peace-keeping units in their armed forces, to be on call to the United Nations, to be specially trained and quickly available, and with advance provision for financial and logistic support.

In addition, the American delegation will suggest a series of steps to improve the United Nations' machinery for the peaceful settlement of disputes, for on-the-spot fact-finding, mediation and adjudication, for extending the rule of inter-national law. For peace is not solely a matter of military or technical problems; it is primarily a problem of politics and people. And unless man can match his strides in weaponry and technology with equal strides in social and political de-velopment, our great strength, like that of the dinosaur, will become incapable of proper control, and man, like the dinosaur, will vanish from the earth.

VI

As we extend the rule of law on earth, so must we also extend it to man's new domain: outer space.

All of us salute the brave cosmonauts of the Soviet Union. The new horizons of outer space must not be riven by the old bitter concepts of imperialism and sovereign claims. The cold reaches of the universe must not become the new arena of an even colder war.

To this end, we shall urge proposals extending the United Nations Charter to the limits of man's exploration in the universe, reserving outer space for peaceful use, prohibiting weapons of mass destruction in space or on celestial bodies, and opening the mysteries and benefits of space to every nation. We shall further propose co-operative efforts in weather prediction and eventually weather control. We shall propose, finally, a global system of communications satellites linking the whole world by telegraph, telephone, radio and television. The day need not be far away when such a system will televise the proceedings of this body to every corner of the world for the benefit of peace.

VII

But the mysteries of outer space must not divert our eyes or our energies from the harsh realities that face our own fellow men. Political sovereignty is but a mockery without the means to meet poverty and illiteracy and disease. Self-determination is but a slogan if the future holds no hope.

That is why my nation, which has freely shared its capital and its technology to help others help themselves, now proposes officially designating this decade of the 1960's as the United Nations Decade of Development. Under the framework of that resolution, the UN's existing efforts in promoting economic growth can be expanded and co-ordinated. Regional surveys and training institutes can pool the talents of many. New research, technical assistance and pilot projects can unlock the wealth of less-developed lands and untapped waters. And development can become a co-operative, not a competitive, enterprise, to enable all nations, however diverse in their systems and beliefs, to become in fact as well as law both free and equal states.

VIII

My country favors a world of free and equal states. We agree with those who say that colonialism is a key issue in this Assembly. But let the full facts of that be discussed in full.

On the one hand is the fact that, since the close of World War II, a world-wide declaration of independence has transformed nearly one billion people and nine million square miles into forty-two free and independent states. Less than 2 per cent of the world's population now lives in "dependent" territories.

I do not ignore the remaining problems of traditional colonialism which still confront this body. Those problems will be solved, with patience, good will and determination. Within the limits of our responsibility in such matters, my country intends to be a participant, not merely an observer, in the peaceful, expeditious movement of nations from the status of colonies to the partnership of equals. That continuing tide of self-determination has our sympathy and our support.

But colonialism in its harshest forms is not only the exploitation of new nations by old, of dark skins by light, or the subjugation of the poor by the rich. My nation was once a colony, and we know what colonialism means: the exploitation and subjugation of the weak by the powerful, of the many by the few, of the governed who have given no consent to be governed, whatever their continent, their class or their color.

And that is why there is no ignoring the fact that the tide of self-determination has not yet reached the Communist empire, where a population far larger than that officially termed "dependent" lives under governments installed by foreign troops instead of free institutions, under a system which knows only one party and one belief, which suppresses free debate, free elections, free newspapers, free books and free trade unions, and which builds a wall to keep truth a stranger and its own citizens prisoners. Let us debate colonialism in full, and apply the principle of free choice and the practice of free plebiscites in every corner of the globe.

IX

Finally, as President of the United States, I consider it my duty to report to this Assembly on two threats to the peace which are not on your crowded agenda, but which cause us, and most of you, the deepest concern.

The first threat on which I wish to report is widely misunderstood: the smoldering coals of war in Southeast Asia. South Vietnam is already under attack, sometimes by a single assassin, sometimes by a band of guerrillas, recently by full battalions. The peaceful borders of Burma, Cambodia and India have been repeatedly violated. And the peaceful people of Laos are in danger of losing the independence they gained not so long ago.

No one can call these "wars of liberation." For these are free countries living under governments of their own choosing. Nor are these aggressions any less real because men are knifed in their homes and not shot in the fields of battle.

The very simple question confronting the world community is whether measures can be devised to protect the small and the weak from such tactics. For if they are successful in Laos and South Vietnam, the gates will be open.

The United States seeks for itself no base, no territory, no special position in this area of any kind. We support a truly neutral and independent Laos, its people free from outside interference, living at peace with themselves and their neighbors, assured that their territory will not be used for attacks on others, and comparable (as Mr. Khrushchev and I agreed at Vienna) to Cambodia and Burma.

But now the negotiations over Laos are reaching a crucial stage. The cease-fire is at best precarious. Laotian territory is being used to infiltrate South Vietnam. The world community must recognize that this potent threat to Laotian peace and freedom is indivisible from all other threats to their own.

Second, I wish to report to you on the crisis over Germany and Berlin. This is not the time or the place for immoderate tones, but the world community is entitled to know the very simple issues as we see them. If there is a crisis it is because an existing peace is under threat, because an existing island of free people is under pressure, because solemn agreements are being treated with contempt. Established international rights are being threatened with unilateral usurpation. Peaceful circulation has been interrupted by barbed wire and concrete blocks.

One recalls the order of the Czar in Pushkin's *Boris Godunov*: "Take steps at this very hour that our frontiers be fenced by barriers . . . that not a single soul pass o'er the border, that not a hare be able to run or a crow to fly."

It is absurd to allege that we are threatening a war merely to prevent the Soviet Union and East Germany from signing a so-called "treaty" of peace. The Western Allies are not concerned with any paper arrangement the Soviets wish to make with a regime of their own creation, on territory occupied by their own troops and governed by their own agents. No such action can affect either our rights or our responsibilities.

If there is a dangerous crisis in Berlin, and there is, it is because of threats against the vital interests and the deep commitments of the Western powers, and the freedom of West Berlin. We cannot yield these interests. We cannot fail these commitments. We cannot surrender the freedom of these people for whom we are responsible. A "peace treaty" which would destroy the peace would be a fraud. A "free city" which was not genuinely free would suffocate freedom and would be an infamy.

For a city or a people to be truly free, they must have the secure right, without economic, political or police pressure, to make their own choice and to live their own lives. And as I have said before, if anyone doubts the extent to which our

presence is desired by the people of West Berlin, we are ready
to have that question submitted to a free vote in all Berlin and,
if possible, among all the German people.

The elementary fact about this crisis is that it is unnecessary.
The elementary tools for a peaceful settlement are found in the
Charter. Under its law, agreements are to be kept, unless
changed by all those who made them. Established rights are to
be respected. The political disposition of peoples should rest
upon their wishes, freely expressed in plebiscites or free elections. If there are legal problems, they can be solved by legal
means. If there is a threat of force, it must be rejected. If there
is desire for change, it must be a subject for negotiation. And if
there is negotiation, it must be rooted in mutual respect and
concern for the rights of others.

The Western powers have calmly resolved to defend, by
whatever means are forced upon them, their obligations and
their access to the free citizens of West Berlin and the self-
determination of those citizens. This generation learned from
bitter experience that either brandishing or yielding to threats
can only lead to war. But firmness and reason can lead to the
kind of peaceful solution in which my country profoundly believes.

We are committed to no rigid formula. We see no perfect
solution. We recognize that troops and tanks can, for a time,
keep a nation divided against its will, however unwise that
policy may be. But we believe a peaceful agreement is possible
which protects the freedom of West Berlin and Allied presence
and access, while recognizing the historic and legitimate interest of others in assuring European security.

The possibilities of negotiation are now being explored; it

is too early to report what the prospects may be. For our part, we will be glad to report at the appropriate time that a solution has been found. For there is no need for a crisis over Berlin, and if those who created this crisis desire peace, there will be peace and freedom in Berlin.

The events and decisions of the next ten months may well decide the fate of man for the next ten thousand years. There will be no avoiding these events. There will be no appeal from these decisions. And we shall be remembered either as the generation that turned this planet into a flaming funeral pyre or the generation that met its vow "to save succeeding generations from the scourge of war."

In the endeavor to meet that vow, I pledge you every effort this nation possesses. I pledge you that we shall neither commit nor provoke aggression, that we shall neither flee nor invoke the threat of force, that we shall never negotiate out of fear and we shall never fear to negotiate.

Terror is not a new weapon. Throughout history it has been used by those who could not prevail either by persuasion or by example. But inevitably they fail, either because men are not afraid to die for a life worth living or because the terrorists themselves come to realize that free men cannot be frightened by threats, and that aggression will meet its own response. And it is in the light of that history that every nation today should know, be he friend or foe, that the United States has both the will and the weapons to join free men in standing up to their responsibilities.

But I come here today to look across this world of threats to the world of peace. In that search we cannot expect any final triumph, for new problems will always arise. We cannot expect that all nations will adopt like systems, for conformity is the jailer of freedom, and the enemy of growth. Nor can we expect to reach our goal by contrivance, by fiat or even by the wishes of all.

But however close we sometimes seem to that dark and final abyss, let no man of peace and freedom despair. For he does not stand alone. If we all can persevere, if we can in every land and office look beyond our own shores and ambitions, then surely the age will dawn in which the strong are just and the weak secure and the peace preserved.

Ladies and gentlemen of this Assembly, the decision is ours. Never have the nations of the world had so much to lose or so much to gain. Together we shall save our planet or together we shall perish in its flames. Save it we can, and save it we must, and then shall we earn the eternal thanks of mankind and, as peacemakers, the eternal blessing of God.

APPENDIX

The following is a list of President Kennedy's statements and addresses included in this book, arranged chronologically. All except for a few major addresses have been shortened. The cuts have been indicated in the texts of the speeches by ellipses.

All the quotations given at the heads of chapters are taken from speeches as they appear in this volume, with the following exceptions:

INDEX

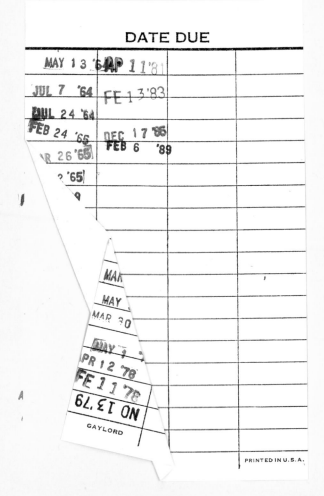

DATE DUE

MAY 13 '64	AP 11'81		
JUL 7 '64	FE 13'83		
JUL 24 '64			
FEB 24 '65	DEC 17 '85		
R 26 '65	FEB 6 '89		
'65			
MAR			
MAY			
MAR 30			
MAY			
PR 12 '78			
FE 11 '78			
NO 13 '79			

GAYLORD

PRINTED IN U.S.A.